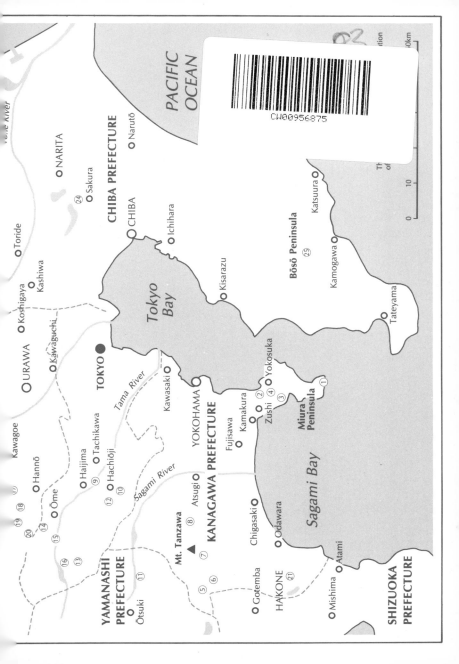

Day Walks Near Tokyo

Day Walks Near Tokyo

by Gary D'A. Walters

KODANSHA INTERNATIONAL
Tokyo and New York

To my walking companions

Cover illustrations by Tarō Higuchi
Maps by Yasunori Yoshida

Distributed in the United States by Kodansha International/
USA Ltd., 114 Fifth Avenue, New York, New York 10011.
Published by Kodansha International Ltd., 2-2 Otowa 1-
chome, Bunkyo-ku, Tokyo 112 and Kodansha International/
USA Ltd., 114 Fifth Avenue, New York, New York 10011.
Copyright © 1988 by Kodansha International Ltd. All rights
reserved. Printed in Japan.
First edition, 1988
Second printing, 1989

Library of Congress Cataloging-in-Publication Data
Walters, Gary D'A.
    Day walks near Tokyo.

    1. Walking—Japan—Tokyo Region—Guide-books.
2. Tokyo Region (Japan)—Description and travel—
Guide-books. I. Title.
GV199.44.J32T659   1988   916.2'135   88-45081
ISBN 0-87011-888-9 (U.S.)
ISBN 4-7700-1388-4 (Japan)

CONTENTS

PREFACE

Towering snow-capped mountains in winter, fast-flowing streams racing through breathtaking ravines in summer, brilliantly colored forests in autumn, an abundance of wildflowers in spring—you could be excused for thinking these to be the Swiss Alps, or at least the Japan Alps. In fact, these sights are only an hour or two away from Tokyo, one of the busiest and most densely populated cities in the world.

Indeed, the Kantō region surrounding Tokyo contains great contrasts in scenery, providing walks in countryside ranging from beachs to rugged mountain, from alpine plateau to river valley, from inland lake to dense native forest. This guide endeavors to introduce walkers to these places by detailing routes that can be completed in single day. Here, the word "walk" rather than "hike" is used, and the paths described are practicable for anyone of reasonable fitness, although the rugged topography of Japan makes for occasional steep climbs.

Twenty-five walks have been selected essentially for their diversity and serenity (in particular, freedom from crowds), and for the richness of native forest they offer. Among the areas covered are parts of the Fuji–Hakone–Izu, Chichibu–Tama, and Nikkō national parks, as well as several prefectural parks, and prefectural and municipal forests. Some of the walks were chosen for their accessibility from Tokyo. In the walk descriptions mention has been made of places of interest, such as temples, shrines, and historical sites, encountered on the way. On most of these walks, a large variety of birds and wildflowers, as well as the occasional wild animal, can be seen. The description of each walk assumes that the reader is not familiar with the Japanese language and provides, hopefully, easy-to-follow instructions, with the Japanese on the signboards reproduced in the text together with the English translation. Readers not familiar with country walking in general are advised to read the introductory sections.

In writing this guide, I have tried to ensure that the route descriptions are as up to date as possible. However, should readers have any comments on the text or their own experiences, I would welcome hearing from them.

Just a few words on the very brief subject of walking etiquette. Do remember to take away your rubbish and the remains of your lunch so that others can also enjoy the forests in their unmarred state. Don't forget to respect general commonsense rules regarding preservation of flora and fauna. And, lastly, it is considered polite to greet other walkers with a *konnichiwa* (good day)!

Acknowledgments

Many people have helped in small by nonetheless essential ways in the preparation of this guide. I am grateful to them all. Ideas for some of the walks originated from Friends of the Earth outings, old *Tokyo Journal* articles, and Keiko Ishikawa. Yasko Tashiro provided some of the translations. Jules Young, the editor, is responsible for that initial encouragement critical to any project. Special thanks are due to Stefan Ottomanski for his suggestions, to Kazuyo Masuda for her enthusiastic and determined tracking down of obscure Japanese place names, and to Suzanne Quan for endless assistance in all aspects.

GARY D'A. WALTERS

INTRODUCTION

Using This Guide

This guide is divided into five initial sections, according to the geographical areas of the Miura Peninsula, Tanzawa, Takao and environs, Okutama, and Okumusashi, with a brief introduction for each section followed by descriptions of four walks. A further five walks in more distant areas (Hakone, Chichibu, Nikkō, Chiba, and the Bōsō Peninsula) are included, making a total of twenty-five walks. The locations of all walks are indicated by their number on the map on the endpapers.

Beside the title of each walk, the letter E (standing for easy), M (for moderate), or D (for relatively difficult) appears. These ratings are based on the length of the walk as well as the steepness of the path, and represent a simple measure of its difficulty to assist the reader in choosing a walk. An appendix at the back of the guide contains additional classifications of suggested walks according to the season, and a list of five recommended walks for the visitor with limited time.

At the beginning of each walk, information is presented under four headings. The first gives a brief outline of the course route, occasionally with alternatives indicated. The second specifies the reference maps that are useful. (Though these are not essential, they give a good perspective of your overall location and are discussed later in this Introduction.) The third heading gives the approximate walking time. Note that the walking times are only intended as a rough guide for two to four "average" walkers, and don't include stops for rests, lunch, and so on. Naturally, actual walking times depend on the individual's pace and the size of the group involved, and considerable time should be allowed for breaks. The fourth and final heading lists features of interest encountered along the way.

Then follows an introductory section, titled "Getting There," which describes the main public transport options for reaching the beginning of the path, including the exact cost at the time of writing. Of course, prices and fares do change, but fortunately around Tokyo this does not occur too often and when there are increases they are usually relatively small. These prices can therefore be considered a reliable guide for the next few years at least. Because timetables for trains and buses are complicated and in many cases subject to seasonal change, I have only provided an indication of the frequency of early morning trains (where expedient or possible), and alternatives to infrequent buses.

As a general compromise to the problem that walkers may set out from different areas of Tokyo, I have usually listed as the starting points either major JR (Japan Railways) Yamanote Line (山手線) stations or their nearby private line counterparts.

For people living in Yokohama, the following lines may be used as convenient short-cuts to get to the start of the walks or to the lines listed in the "Getting There" sections:

To Hakone: JR Tōkaidō Line (東海道線) to Odawara (小田原).

To Tanzawa: JR Tōkaidō Line to Fujisawa (藤沢), then Odakyū Enoshima Line (小田急江ノ島線) to Sagami-Ōno (相模大野).

To Takao and environs: JR Yokohama Line (横浜線) to Hachiō-ji (八王子), and JR Yokohama and Hachikō (八高線) Lines to Komiya (小宮).

To Okutama: JR Yokohama and Hachikō Lines to Haijima (拝島).

To Okumusashi: JR Yokohama and Hachikō Lines to Higashi-Hannō (東飯能), and JR Yokohama and Hachikō Lines to Ogose (越生).

To Chichibu: JR Yokohama and Hachikō Lines to Higashi-Hannō.

The description of each walk is broken into two or three linking route segments (between stations, bus stops and landmarks), each with its own total walking time indicated. The signposts you encounter as you walk present something of a problem, in as much as the Japanese may be written from left to right, from top to bottom, or, occasionally, from right to left. In the first two cases, I have presented the Japanese (in parentheses after the translation and/or romanized Japanese) in the order from left to right, but in the third case I have retained the right to left order, hopefully to avoid confusing people with little knowledge of Japanese, since that is how they will see it. The English language terms "path," "trail," and "track" have been used synonymously.

The times given for sloping paths are only pertinent to the direction of travel that is described, whether uphill or downhill. Snow-covered or muddy terrain will increase these times considerably. Information regarding alternative (including shortened) routes and the directions of other paths from intersections is provided where useful or of interest. Since landmarks change with time—new roads and housing estates are constructed, signs disappear (and are sometimes added!), and so on—remember to be flexible and use a little common sense if some description no longer seems to match the terrain.

Each walk is accompanied by a detailed sketch map that includes the many minor trails branching off; the sketch map and description are intended to be read in conjunction. Note that the scale used on the sketch map is only an indication of the distances involved and should not be used as an accurate measure of short distances, since some parts of the indicated route may be distorted to show certain features more clearly. The symbols used in these sketch maps are:

- - - The Route of the Walk
— Other Walking Track
▬ Road
■□ / ╫╫ Railway
• Bus Stop
卍 Temple
开 Shrine
▲ Mountain/Peak
♨ Spa

Preparing for Walks

Although one-day walks do not require a great deal of preparation, a few things can be done to make them more enjoyable. These include obtaining a suitable pack, clothing and footwear; taking sufficient food and drink; and adequate planning beforehand with respect to maps, and travel and walking times to ensure that the walk can be completed within a day. These aspects are covered below.

PACKS

A good pack is essential to hold all the items you need and to free your hands for other purposes such as reading maps and guides, photography, birdwatching, as well as maintaining balance. Probably the best kind of pack is a larger version of the waterproof, frameless day-packs commonly used by Japanese children when they go on excursions. It should feel comfortable when loaded.

CLOTHING

The main requirement is to dress suitably for the season, taking into account that temperatures can drop fairly rapidly, especially near the summit of a windswept mountain, whereas, equally importantly, exertion results in the body heating up. It is, therefore, better to dress in layers that can be easily removed or added to. A warm jacket and gloves are absolutely essential in winter, and a light waterproof jacket or, at the very least, a pullover is a good idea at any time of the year. Jackets with a pocket large enough to hold a map or guidebook are best, since repeatedly reaching into a pack for these can become annoying. Winter and summer hats are also recommended to reduce heat loss and sunburn/sunstroke, respectively. If you intend to stop at an *onsen* (hot spring), don't forget to take a small towel.

FOOTWEAR

Although many day walkers can be seen wearing running shoes or the like, these can be inadequate for the tougher walks described in this book. On the other hand, expensive hiking boots are not worth purchasing unless you also intend to use them for longer, more arduous hikes. The best compromise is a pair of sturdy walking shoes or ankle-height hiking boots (without lace-up gaiters) that provide good support on inclines. Choose good quality leather or nylon-mesh boots that allow your feet to "breathe." As with all shoes, walking boots should be worn in before being used on a long walk, and should be washed clean of dirt afterwards to prevent deterioration.

FOOD AND DRINK

A hearty breakfast is a good prelude to a day's walk—it will have plenty of time to settle before you reach the start of the trail. Although the food to eat during a walk is a matter of personal taste, it should be nourishing—Japanese *bentō* (boxed lunches) and *onigiri* (rice balls) sold near railway stations make convenient lunches—and sufficient, since food is rarely available along the route. Some walkers feel that a series of light snacks is better than one large meal. In any case, something to provide a little energy late in the afternoon comes in handy.

As for drinks, the "sports" formulas are very good in summer, whereas hot drinks go a long way toward reviving flagging spirits in winter. In addition to these, a container (preferably of the light, collapsible type) of drinking water should be carried. Again, canned drinks and water are generally not available along the route, and should be obtained from railway stations or near the start of the walk.

MAPS AND TIME PLANNING

The sketch maps that accompany each walk should suffice, so the maps mentioned under the heading "Reference map" are not strictly required. However, they are useful in determining the route if some change in the landscape has occurred, as well as for the various reasons given below.

In the absence of English-language material, the most suitable walking maps of Japan are the Japanese-language Nitchi Series of *Tozan haikingu* (ニッチ登山ハイキングシリーズ, "Mountain Climbing and Hiking") and Shōbunsha's *Yama to Kōgen* (昭文社/山と高原地図, "Mountain and Plateau"). The original series of both have recently been replaced with new series with nearly identical maps and a price of ¥600. The relevant numbers of the new and old maps for both series are listed at the beginning of each walk description.

Also useful are the large-scale (1:25,000) Geographical Survey Institute (国土地理院) sheet maps, which cost ¥220. Although the larger scale of the sheet maps makes them helpful for some walks, the Nitchi and Shōbunsha series have the advantages of displaying better the more recognized walking trails and giving details of bus connections to the paths. All of these publications are available from major bookstores.

The easiest method of finding your way around these maps is to use the map's main landmark index, or, if there is none, to locate the appropriate railway line and then let your eye follow this to the station mentioned. From there, you should be able to find a key element of the walking course, such as a major mountain, or a road leading to the bus stop (in the case of the Nitchi and Shōbunsha maps, often marked in red in a small box and approximately identifiable by the time given) at the start of the walk.

When using a map and compass, the map should be laid horizontal and then rotated to align its north marker with the compass needle. Subsequently, landmarks can be identified with respect to your own position from the direction indicated by the map.

Although the task of time planning, that is, determining a route whose times (including travel) are realistic for a single day, has already been undertaken for the walks in this guide, it is essential to start out early, preferably between 6 and 7 A.M., depending on your starting point, to allow for poor train and bus connections and delays. Keeping an eye on the time while walking is important, as mountain paths become dangerous as darkness falls (which happens quite early in winter) and bus services usually cease operating at about 6 or 7 P.M., or even earlier. Six hours of walking is considered a comfortable limit.

Transportation

TRAINS

The destination, type, and departure time of trains (in addition to being announced in Japanese) are often displayed on an overhead sign just inside the ticket barrier, particularly in the large terminus stations of Tokyo. This sign also usually lists the next few trains and the platforms they leave from. Otherwise, train information can be obtained from the sign or the timetable near or on the appropriate platform. A final check of the destination may be made by looking at the front (and sometimes the side) of the train itself. The type of train (express, limited express, etc.) is sometimes displayed on the front of the train, at other times on the side.

The timetables themselves are rather more complex affairs, with different symbols used to mark destinations and train types. Note that 平日 (often in blue) refers to Monday to Saturday, while 休日 (red) is for Sundays and public holidays.

For some walks, the possibility of catching faster trains with a surcharge is described. The basic ticket is known as a *jōshaken* (passenger ticket), and the supplementary fare as a *tokkyūken* (limited express ticket). Purchasing a *tokkyūken* does not necessarily entitle you to a reserved seat (known as *shiteiseki*), which may cost a little more. In trains with reserved seats, however, there are usually also carriages with unreserved seating.

BUSES

Unlike Tokyo city buses, which you usually board at the front, paying a fixed fare as you get on, longer-distance country buses have their entrance at the rear or middle, and the fare, which depends on the distance traveled, is paid when you get off (at the front door). Except when you board at the terminus (or in the first sector of the route), you should take a ticket from the machine next to the steps as you board. The number on this ticket is later used to determine your fare from the illuminated board visible at the front of the bus near the driver. Most buses referred to in this guide are of this variable-fare type.

Note that different timetables often apply for weekdays/ Saturdays and Sundays/public holidays, as with trains.

For many hiking areas near Tokyo, passes are available that permit travel to and from, as well as within, the area—*jiyūkippu* (freedom tickets) are usually only valid for trains, while *furiipasu* (free passes) frequently include use of buses and cable cars for sightseeing. Most of these are only worthwhile if you spend the weekend in the area and move around a lot. The most useful of these for the day walks is suggested in the appropriate section.

The total cost of transport (train and, if applicable, bus) for the walks described in this guide ranges from ¥680 to ¥4,890, with an average of about ¥1,800.

Safety

Since most of the routes in this guide are not too far away from at least a farmhouse, should you lose your way there is little cause for worry if you use your common sense. Care is definitely needed on paths up steep slopes or across ridges with adjacent sheer drops. Occasionally in summer, basking snakes can be a hazard. Any potential dangers of going on walks can be minimized by taking the following steps:

1. Check the weather forecast before leaving home. If rain is likely, postpone the walk. Slippery slopes in areas such as Tanzawa and Okutama can be treacherous. Avoid walking in excessively hot conditions or in remote regions with heavy snow cover.

2. Take a map and compass. If you lose your way, these may be of help in providing some idea of your location from the map contours and surrounding landmarks.

3. Take sufficient food and drink in case the walk lasts longer than expected. Waterproof matches for lighting fires and a flashlight are sensible emergency items to carry.

4. Don't walk alone. Three adults is usually considered the minimum safe number. Stay together and make sure all members of the group have a copy of the route.

5. Take plenty of rests, and travel at a pace comfortable for the slowest member of the group. It is also wise to pace yourself by not walking too fast too early, and by slowing down on steep ascents.

6. Let someone know where you are going and, of course, inform them on your return.

Emergency Japanese

Generally, you will find that Japanese people are not only friendly and helpful but also that many of them, particularly city people (who are often fellow walkers), can speak a little English. However, should you have difficulty in making yourself understood, the following basic words and phrases will assist you in obtaining directions, identifying landmarks, and communicating in case of emergency. For these, the Hepburn system, in which so-called long "o" and "u" vowels are denoted by a bar above the vowel, has been used. (The vowel sounds are approximately: "a" as in the first syllable of "banana," "e" as in "egg," "i" as in "pin," "o" as in "hot," and "u" as in "put.")

Mt. . . . . . .*yama* or . . .*san* (*zan*) 山
. . . Peak . . .*mine* 峰 or 嶺
. . . Hill (Peak) . . .*tsuka* (*zuka*) 塚
. . . Pass . . .*tōge* 峠
Lake . . . . . .*ko* 湖
. . . River . . .*kawa* (*gawa*) 川
Cape . . . . . .*saki* (*zaki*) 崎
. . . Temple . . .*tera* (*dera*) or . . .*ji* 寺
. . . Shrine . . .*jinja* 神社
station *eki* 駅
bus stop *basu tei* バス停
direction *hōmen* 方面
left *hidari* 左
right *migi* 右
straight on *massugu* まっすぐ
toilet *otearai* 御手洗 or お手洗
thank you *arigatō* ありがとう

Does this train/bus go to . . .?
Kono densha/basu wa . . . e ikimasu ka?
この電車/バスは…へ行きますか.

Please tell me when we reach . . .
. . . ni tsuitara oshiete kudasai.
…に着いたら教えて下さい.

Is this the way to . . .?
Kochira wa . . . hōmen desu ka?
こちらは…方面ですか.

I am/my friend is sick/injured.
Watashi/tomodachi wa byoki desu/kega shimashita.
私/友達は病気です/ケガしました.

Birdwatching and Wildflower Field Guides

Birdwatchers need look no further than the excellent *A Field Guide to the Birds of Japan*, by the Wild Bird Society of Japan (published by the Wild Bird Society of Japan in cooperation with Kodansha International Ltd., 1986), and *Finding Birds in Japan: The Tokyo Area*, by Mark Brazil. Both of these publications were used in the preparation of this guidebook. If the latter is not available, *A Birdwatcher's Guide to Japan*, by Mark Brazil (published by Kodansha International Ltd. in cooperation with the Wild Bird Society of Japan, 1987) will be a useful substitute.

Wildflower enthusiasts, however, are not so fortunate, although there is a wealth of Japanese-language material, including field guides according to season, region, and type of plant. The flowers named in this book were identified using the comprehensive, well-illustrated references *Nihon no nohana* (日本の野草) (Wildflowers of Japan; Yama-kei, 1983) and *Nihon no jumoki* (日本の樹木) (Woody Plants of Japan; Yama-kei, 1985).

Further Walking

Unfortunately, there is virtually no detailed English-language publication on hiking near Tokyo other than this guide, although a small book on hiking areas in Japan as a whole has been published. However, if some degree of confidence can be developed with the hiking maps mentioned, the possibilities are endless. A quick glance at some of these maps will show the many red lines representing walking trails, as well as access to the walks by bus and train.

The walks in this guide are of the one-day kind, but if you have time two-day walks are equally feasible, although more preparation and planning are required. For such walks, it is possible to stay overnight in mountain cabins, the locations of which are also marked on some walking maps.

Another possibility is to join a walking club or organization that has walking as one of its regular activities. Such groups in Tokyo include Friends of the Earth, Tel. (03)770-6308, and the International Adventure Club, Tel. (03)333-0419 or (03) 327-2905, which include both Japanese and foreign members. Even if you don't wish to walk regularly with a number of people, these group walks can open up new vistas to you.

Happy walking!

MIURA PENINSULA

Miura, the part of Kanagawa Prefecture to the south of Tokyo, juts out into the Pacific Ocean and, together with the Bōsō Peninsula, forms Tokyo Bay. The last remnants of untouched forest and coast on this otherwise heavily populated peninsula provide probably the greatest range of walking country close to Tokyo, from seaside stroll to mountain ascent, and are excellent for the less adventurous walker.

The Keihin Kyūkō Line (from Shinagawa) and its associated branches serve most areas, with the JR Yokosuka Line an alternative in some cases.

1. CAPE TSURUGI ————————————————— E

Course: Miura-kaigan Station (by bus) → Togari → Cape Tsurugi Lighthouse ⌐→ Matsuwa-kaigan (by bus) → Miura-kaigan Station
└→ Jō Island (by bus) → Misaki-guchi Station

Reference map: Nitchi Map No. 12 (Miura hantō, 三浦半島), New Series No. 28.

Walking time: About 3 hours (excluding alternative route).

Points of interest: Rugged coastline and sea views, Cape Tsurugi Lighthouse, caves, and seaweed cultivation.

Note: At high tide, the route may be impassable, if not dangerous. Approximate times of high and low tides can be found in the daily newspapers.

GETTING THERE

From Shinagawa Station, take a Keihin Kyūkō Line (京浜急行線) limited express (*tokkyū*, 特急) or a slightly faster and more comfortable rapid limited express (*kaisoku tokkyū*, 快速特急) bound for Misaki-guchi (三崎口). The last part of the journey actually runs

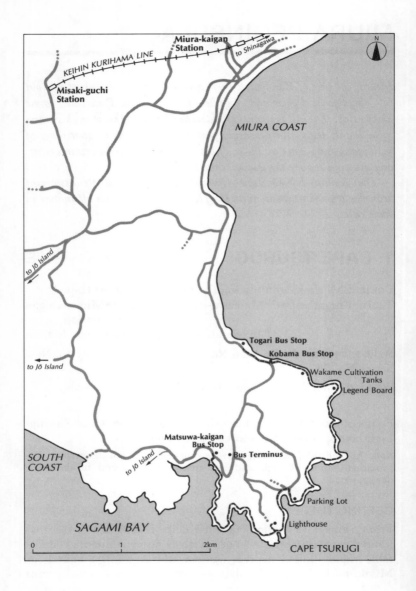

along the Keihin Kurihama Line (京浜久里浜線), but no transfer is needed. Get off at Miura-kaigan (三浦海岸) Station, the second from last stop.

Rapid limited expresses take just over 1 hour to reach Miura-kaigan; limited expresses take 1 hour and 14 minutes; and other, slower trains considerably longer. The fare in all cases is ¥660.

Leave the station by the only exit, walk slightly to the right to Bus Stand No. 2, and board a bus bound for Cape Tsurugi (*Tsurugizaki*, 剣崎). The bus route runs along the shoreline, providing good views of this beach that is popular with windsurfers. After about 12 minutes, get off at Togari (鋒). The fare is ¥200.

From Togari to Cape Tsurugi Lighthouse (2 hours 15 minutes)

Walk along the road or the beach in the same direction as the bus was traveling. The smell of the sea, the cry of gulls, and the fishing boats and nets all make for a pleasant atmosphere. In less than 10 minutes, you will reach Kobama (小浜) Bus Stop. Just beyond the stop, a small road veers downhill toward the sea. Follow this past several buildings and beached boats to the base of the cliff, where you will find a small path.

This path follows the edge of the shore past fishnet racks and sheds. Among the wildflowers common to this coast are small blue *tsuyukusa* (dayflower or spiderwort) in late spring and early summer, and in summer and autumn tiny pink *mamakonoshirinugui* (polygonum knotweed), purple *hamabenogiku* (daisy), *azami* (thistle), *hototogisu* (*Tricyrtis hirta*, also known as toad lily), white *fujibakama* (eupatorium thoroughwort), and yellow *ōmatsuyoigusa* (oenothera evening primrose).

Soon you will come to some small structures containing tanks for the cultivation of *wakame*, a kind of seaweed. The spores are grown in these tanks and, when large enough, are transferred to the sea for maturation.

In a tiny cove some 15–20 minutes from Kobama Bus Stop, you will find holiday houses and sailing boats. After a further 10 minutes, you reach a large, decaying signboard recounting the legend of *Amezaki no orochi*, a large mythical snake once much feared by local people, who tried to be quiet in this area to avoid arousing it.

At this point, leave the trail, drop down to the sand, and follow the beach to the continuation of the path at the base of the cliffs. The remainder of the walk is on paths that skirt the bottom of the cliffs and cross the beaches of several small bays, or that are cut out of the rock face, in some places with concrete sections and circular stepping stones to facilitate traversing difficult parts. In some bays are multicolored *nobudō*, a kind of wild but inedible grapelike berry. Birds to look for include cormorants, egrets, kites, sandpipers, water pipits, daurian redstarts, and blue rock thrushes. Also interesting are the sedimentary and fault lines of the cliff faces.

The next headland, like many places along this coast, is very popular with fishermen. Some 15 minutes from the legend board, you cross a small beach, curve around more cliffs, and then after another 15 minutes pass through a little fishing and agricultural village. In late September, the edges of the fields are ablaze with scarlet *higanbana* (cluster amaryllis).

Continue by following the path by the cliff at the other end of the beach. Around this next promontory, the pounding of the waves on the rocks results in towering columns of spray that can

"Waterfall" resulting from depressions in a rocky shelf.

be quite spectacular. Be warned, though, that it can be extremely dangerous to get too close to these rocks, which are periodically engulfed by waves. This is a good place to sit and have lunch while you watch the ships and the birds.

From here you have to pass along a very narrow, eroded ledge. If this seems too difficult, try descending to the rocks below and going that way. Next, you have to negotiate either a small "bridge," which is regularly washed by waves at high tide, or the nearby cliff path. Here you will see large rectangular holes carved out of the rock that were used for making salt.

In 15 minutes you reach a bay with a village and a beach. Like several of Cape Tsurugi's beaches, there are large signs instructing people to beware of tsunami, or tidal waves, that sometimes follow large earthquakes. Other signs seen along the trail are those warning of the danger of falling rocks.

At the next cliff, there is again a small ledge, though this time quite easy to pass. As you round the headland, you see a large dirt parking lot and a small harbor just beyond, with Cape Tsurugi Lighthouse in the distance. The harbor can be reached in 15 minutes from the previous bay. Cross the parking lot and follow the road that runs parallel with the waterfront past the boats to the other side of the harbor. The track winds around a point, crosses a small beach, and then continues along the base of more cliffs. The beaches on this walk, incidentally, are testimony to the dire need for all people—walkers, picnickers, or local residents—to take their rubbish away with them.

After passing two tiny "islands," which can actually be reached on foot from the mainland, you come to a small bay. The path to the lighthouse leads uphill from here. *Hamakanzō* (orange lilies), usually found near the sea, are common in late summer and early autumn here. Straight ahead are fields of *daikon* (Japanese giant radish), for which the Miura Peninsula is famous. About halfway up, turn right onto the paved path that zigzags to the top. It takes 30–35 minutes from the harbor to the lighthouse.

The lighthouse is quite old, as shown by a sign that proudly announces, in English, "Illuminated 1st March 1871," and though you cannot enter it, you can walk around the grounds and enjoy the view across to the Bōsō Peninsula.

At this point, it is possible to shorten the walk by taking the road for about 20 minutes from the lighthouse to the main road, where the terminus for the Cape Tsurugi bus that you boarded at Miura-kaigan Station is located. To return to Miura-kaigan Station, board the bus here.

From Cape Tsurugi Lighthouse to Matsuwa-kaigan (45 minutes)

To complete the entire walk, return to the small bay by the same path you came up, noting the covered old well on the right about halfway down the slope. Continue around the coast on more cliff-side trails past several giant caves. At one point a large rocky shelf projects out to sea. The various depressions in this shelf collect water from the waves as they are trapped on the western side and drain across to the eastern side, where the water pours like a waterfall back into the ocean. If the water level is high, you may have to remove your shoes to walk through the pools.

About 40 minutes after leaving the lighthouse, and just before reaching another town, you pass more seaweed cultivation facilities. Go around the gate and follow the small road to where it meets the main road. Turn left and walk 50 meters or so down the road, and Matsuwa-kaigan Bus Stop is on the right. The bus to Miura-kaigan Station takes 25 minutes. The fare is ¥250. If the bus timetable at the stop shows a very long wait for the next bus, simply walk up the road, in the direction the bus would go, to the terminus for the Cape Tsurugi bus. From Miura-kaigan Station, return to Tokyo via Shinagawa. Some trains only go as far as Keihin-Kurihama Station, where you cross to the other side of the platform to catch the next train to Shinagawa.

Cape Tsurugi Lighthouse to Jō Island (3 hours 15 minutes)

If you have the time and energy, it is possible to extend the walk from Cape Tsurugi Lighthouse all the way to Jō Island (*Jōgashima*, 城ヶ島). Follow the road past Matsuwa-kaigan Bus Stop and out of town. Part of the way up the first slope is a break in the white guard rail on the left side. Take the path that leads down from here to cross some marshy ground to the edge of the sea. In roughly 2 hours 30 minutes, you will arrive at the huge elevated bridge across to Jō Island. The stairs under the bridge are reached by way of the back streets of Harumi-chō. After crossing the bridge, take the path immediately to the right, make your way through the maze of tracks, and get on a dirt road to the headland on the opposite side of the island. Steps lead down to the beach on the left. At the far end of the beach, large numbers of *umiu* (Temminck's cormorant) can usually be seen. To return home, climb the steps and descend to the beach on the other side of the headland. Walk along the coast until you reach a town. The walk from the bridge to this point takes about 45 minutes. Take the road through the market to Jōgashima bus terminus, where you should catch a bus bound for Misaki-guchi Station, which is also on the Keihin Kyūkō Line to Shinagawa. The 30-minute ride costs ¥330.

Cliffside trail along Cape Tsurugi.

2. JIMMU TEMPLE ——————————————— E

Course: Jimmu-ji Station → Jimmu Temple → Mt. Takatori → Keihin-Taura Station

Reference map: Nitchi Map No. 12 (Miura hantō, 三浦半島), New Series No. 28.

Walking time: About 1 hour 50 minutes.

Points of interest: Jimmu Temple and the nearby rock-climbing practice area.

GETTING THERE

The most direct means is by an express (*kyūkō*, 急行) on the Keihin Kyūkō Line (京浜急行線) from Shinagawa Station to Jimmu-ji (神武寺) Station. This is actually the second station on a small branch line, known as the Zushi Line (逗子線), which leaves the main tracks at Kanazawa-Hakkei (金沢八景) Station. Since most trains from Shinagawa follow the main line, make sure your train is bound for Shin-Zushi (新逗子) Station (the terminus of the Zushi Line), or else you have to change trains. In this case, take a faster limited express (*tokkyū*, 特急) or the still faster and more comfortable rapid limited express (*kaisoku tokkyū*, 快速特急), and transfer at Kanazawa-Bunko (金沢文庫) Station to a local train bound for Shin-Zushi. Get off at Jimmu-ji Station. Local trains can leave from either side of the platform.

A direct express to Jimmu-ji Station takes just over 1 hour, while the two legs of the alternative require about 35 minutes for the rapid limited express and 7 minutes for the local train. The fare in either case is ¥460.

From Jimmu-ji Station to Jimmu Temple (50 minutes)

Leave Jimmu-ji Station by the only exit and follow the short lane to the main road. Turn left, and in about 7–8 minutes, at the second set of traffic lights, you will see a small road leading to the right beside a high school sports ground. This sport ground is surrounded by trees, but the corner where you turn is clearly identified by a telephone booth and a noticeboard with a map showing the route to Jimmu Temple (*Jimmu-ji*, 神武寺). Follow this small road, which skirts some hills, for another 7–8 minutes until it stops at a block of apartments. A reasonably wide walking path continues almost straight ahead.

Near the start of this path are, on the right, a park with fish ponds and miniature trees, or *bonsai*, and, a little farther on the left, a rockface that has been quarried. The path is extremely picturesque, if a little strenuous, as it meanders uphill between mossy boulders along the bed of a small stream. In some places the old stone steps leading to Jimmu Temple still remain, and the surrounding rocky slopes are covered with ferns. This area is a wildlife protection zone.

After about 10 minutes, a small path leads off to the left, but ignore this and go right toward Jimmu Temple, as indicated by the sign. Some 15–20 minutes later there is another fork with a signpost: ahead lies the Main Hall (本堂) of Jimmu Temple, while the right-hand route leads to Higashi-Zushi (東逗子) Station on the JR Yokosuka Line (横須賀線).

Walk straight on, pass under a roofed gateway, and climb the stone steps. At the top of these is a bell platform with dragons carved on the ends of the wooden ceiling joists. Below and to the left are some modern buildings, including the priests' quarters and a pond belonging to the temple; below and to the right, above a new road, is a graveyard. Up another flight of steps lie the principal temple buildings, including a magnificent entranceway and the Main Hall, as well as the foundations and some stone columns of a gateway (*torii*) that was leveled by the Great Kantō Earthquake of 1923. Stone figures of Jizō, adorned with red berets and bibs as befits the guardian deity of children, can also be seen in the temple grounds.

Although the temple is said to date back to the eighth century and the well-known Buddhist monk Gyōgi (668–749), its more certain history can be traced to 1590, when many samurai fleeing from Hideyoshi's siege of Odawara Castle took refuge here. The pursuing army burned down the Main Hall, but it was soon reconstructed, though appropriately smaller so as not to invite further attention. The roof still has the traditional thatch of *susuki* (pampas grass).

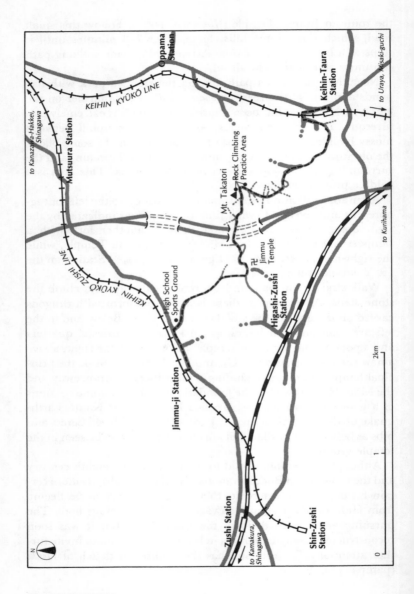

Jimmu Temple's more recent claim to fame is the frequent visits of Emperor Hirohito, who in his younger days as Crown Prince would stay and collect mold specimens for his botanical studies. The room he used has been preserved as it was then. The temple previously contained some of the finer Buddhist relics in the Kamakura region, and these are now occasionally displayed at the Kamakura National Museum, near Hachiman Shrine, not far from Kamakura Station.

In fact, the walk to Jimmu Temple and a visit to Kamakura can easily be combined. To do so, return to the fork with the signpost and take the path leading to Higashi-Zushi Station. The track is quite rocky, but it is downhill, and in less than 10 minutes you pass between some buildings and, a few minutes later, reach a road. Follow this downhill until it meets the main road, turn left and walk to the station by crossing the tracks. Kamakura is two stations, or 9 minutes, away. Alternatively, return to Tokyo via Shinagawa Station, which is on the same line (57 minutes, ¥680).

From Jimmu Temple to Keihin-Taura Station (1 hour)

At the back of the temple, to the left, are steps with a signpost for Mt. Takatori (*Takatoriyama*, 鷹取山), signaling the next stage of the walk. After a short climb, the path traverses a series of ridges, with spectacular views of both sides of the Miura Peninsula and the surrounding sea. In reasonably fine conditions, you can also see the Bōsō Peninsula on the other side of Tokyo Bay. If you go looking for good vantage points, beware of sheer drops at the end of short tracks, particularly on the right side. Keep on the clearly marked trail to Mt. Takatori and ignore the paths leading downhill to the left. This trail passes several electricity pylons and crosses directly over a highway, which is visible on either side of the path where it emerges from a tunnel.

Within 20 minutes of leaving Jimmu Temple, you enter an old quarry overlooked by a communications installation on the summit of Mt. Takatori. On weekends, the quarry walls are popular with rock and mountain climbers practicing in groups. The uninterrupted vistas and sheltered location make this a favorite lunch spot for hikers.

From the quarry viewing area, enclosed within railings, walk in

Rock climbing below the summit of Mt. Takatori.

the same general direction as when you entered the quarry, toward a gap in the walls. A few meters on the other side of this gap is a fork with a signpost. Take the right-hand path, which leads "to Keihin-Taura Station" (至京浜田浦駅) on the Keihin Kyūkō Line. (The other path is marked "至磨仏.")

This will bring you to the station in about 45 minutes. Stay on the main track as it winds along the ridges, keeping an eye open for the signs pointing toward the station. Although houses can be seen below on the left for the remainder of the walk, this is a very pretty path, with a fern-filled forest on the right.

About 20 minutes after leaving the quarry and shortly after passing some electricity pylons, the path ends at a small road leading downhill to the left. A sign here indicates that this is also the direction of Keihin-Taura Station. Follow the road for 50 meters or so until it meets another road. Veer right and walk along this road for about 100 meters until it ends, then go down the track that lies straight ahead. Some small fields are on the left.

In about 10 minutes, to the left of a junction with a signpost, the station should be visible below. Take the left-hand path down to the bitumen road. Since the sole station entrance is on the other side of the tracks, you have to follow this road to a T-junction, turn right under the railway bridge, turn right again at the main road, and walk back to the station.

Return to Tokyo via Shinagawa Station (¥460).

3. MT. ŌGUSU

Course: Shin-Zushi Station (by bus) → Maedabashi → Mt. Ōgusu → Ōgusu-tozan-guchi (by bus) → Shin-Zushi Station

Reference map: Nitchi Map No. 12 (Miura hantō, 三浦半島), New Series No. 28.

Walking time: About 2 hours.

Points of interest: The variety of trees, including many identified with labels, and abundant birds and wildflowers in broad-leaved evergreen forest.

GETTING THERE

The most direct means is by a Keihin Kyūkō Line (京浜急行線) express (kyūkō, 急行) from Shinagawa Station to Shin-Zushi (新逗子) Station. Shin-Zushi is actually the terminus of a small branch line called the Zushi Line (逗子線), which leaves the main tracks at Kanazawa-Hakkei (金沢八景) Station. Since most trains from Shinagawa follow the main line, make sure that your train is bound for Shin-Zushi, or else you have to change trains. In this case, take a faster limited express (tokkyū, 特急) or the still faster and more comfortable rapid limited express (kaisoku tokkyū, 快速特急), and transfer at Kanazawa-Bunko (金沢文庫) Station to the local train for Shin-Zushi. This can leave from either side of the platform.

A direct express to Shin-Zushi takes about 64 minutes, while the two legs of the alternative require about 35 minutes for the rapid limited express and 10 minutes for the local train. The fare in either case is ¥510.

Leave Shin-Zushi Station by the south exit, which is nearest the front of the train as you arrive, go to the road a few meters to your right and turn left. Walk 50 meters or so to Bus Stand No. 1 and catch a bus bound for Nagai (長井) or Yokosuka Station (横須賀駅). Part of the ride skirts the west coast of the Miura Peninsula. After 20–25 minutes, get off at Maedabashi (前田橋) Bus Stop. The fare is ¥300.

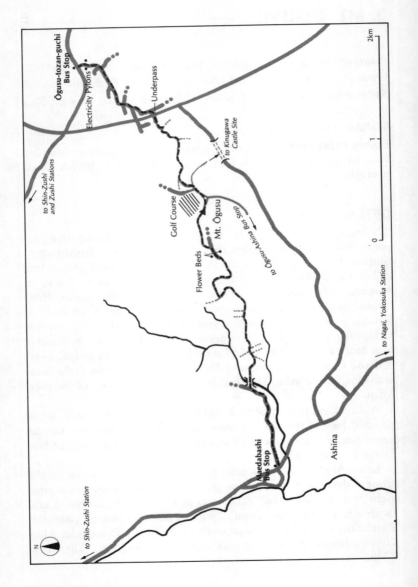

From Maedabashi to Mt. Ōgusu (1 hour 10 minutes)

Just past the bus stop, by a map signboard, is a lane to the left. Follow this between houses and fields for about 10 minutes until the road surface changes to dirt. Some 20 meters farther on, turn right over a small bridge. A signpost there indicates the way to Mt. Ōgusu (*Ōgusuyama*, 大楠山). The path immediately leads up some steps and in places runs through a steep, rocky hollow eroded out of a fern-covered slope. Ignore any lesser paths veering off the main trail. Concrete benches have been set up at regular intervals.

The ascent and the trail down the other side of Mt. Ōgusu pass through beech and oak forest. Many trees beside the path bear labels in Japanese katakana script for the benefit of visitors. Some of these are: アカガシ (*akagashi*, a Japanese evergreen oak), アスナロ (*asunaro*, which is *Hiba arborvitae*, an ornamental evergreen), エゴノキ (*egonoki*, snowbell or storax), エノキ (*enoki*, Chinese nettle or hackberry), ハコネウツギ (*hakoneutsugi*, bush honeysuckle), ハゼ (*haze*, sumac or wax tree, the leaves of which are used in tanning and dyeing), カエデ (*kaede*, a kind of maple), ケヤキ (*keyaki*, zelkova), キブシ (*kibushi*, *Stachyurus praecox*), クヌギ (*kunugi*, another type of oak), クスノキ (*kusunoki*, camphor or laurel), マユミ (*mayumi*, spindle tree), オオシマザクラ (*ōshimazakura*, Ōshima cherry), and スギ (*sugi*, cedar).

The path subsequently levels off and follows the line of a ridge, winding at times through areas of dwarf bamboo (*sasa*). Wildflowers common here include various kinds of daisy and violet in early spring, and *tsuyukusa* (spiderwort) and *kuzu* (arrowroot) in late summer and early autumn. Birds such as kites and long-tailed tits are common in the forest.

After 30–35 minutes, turn right at a T-junction with a sign indicating the direction of Mt. Ōgusu. About 20 minutes later you come to a dirt road leading through a large clearing used for cultivating flowers. In early spring, *nanohana* (rape, whose stems and yellow flowers are boiled and eaten) are grown here, and in summer, white, pink, and red *kosumosu* (cosmos) flourish.

Walk along the dirt road between the flowerbeds to 50 to 100 meters past a steel tower, where a trail marked for Mt. Ōgusu leads uphill to the left. A few minutes up this track is the summit

Steps up through a rocky hollow mark the start of the path.

of Mt. Ōgusu, which has an observation platform and several communications towers. A golf course can be seen to the northwest, and the 360° panorama of Miura Peninsula, not to mention the benches, make this a suitable place to have lunch.

From Mt. Ōgusu to Ōgusu-tozan-guchi (50 minutes)

On the other side of the summit, the path descends via a series of steep steps. In 5 minutes you reach a T-junction. The right-hand track leads to Ōgusu-Ashina Bus Stop about 50 minutes away, but turn left here, toward the site of Kinugawa Castle (衣笠城址). Follow the trail along the edge of the golf course until, after about 10 minutes and some 50 meters beyond the corner of the course boundary, you arrive at another T-junction, with a track to the left marked for Abekura Spa (*Abekura onsen*, 阿部倉温泉). Take this path down more steep steps, past a tower, and through forest. At the bottom is a pretty stream with fern-covered banks. Stay on the main path, which meanders over several bridges and below a stand of tall bamboo on the left, in the direction of Tsukayama Park (*Tsukayama koen*, 塚山公園).

The trail to Mt. Ōgusu.

Some 15–20 minutes from the second T-junction, the path becomes a road that crosses under a highway. The bus stop is only 15 minutes from here.

Turn left at the T-junction on the other side of the highway and continue along this bitumen road around the corner and up the hill to where it meets another road. Turn right toward Tsukayama Park and then, shortly after, left along a prefectural road (県道) that winds down the hill. Ignore the small roads to the left. A road soon merges from the right and another leads off nearby, again to the left, but continue straight on, between two electricity pylons and down to the main road. Ōgusu-tozan-guchi Bus Stop is immediately on your left. Catch a bus bound for Zushi Station (逗子駅) and get off at Shin-Zushi Eki (新逗子駅) Bus Stop. This takes 25 minutes and the fare is ¥330.

After leaving the bus, cross the road and walk down the road branching off at the nearby T-junction to Shin-Zushi Station, which is about 100 meters away. Return to Shinagawa by following in reverse the instructions given in the "Getting There" section.

4. MT. FUTAGO ———————————— M

Course: Shin-Zushi Station → Mt. Futago → Taura Station

Reference map: Nitchi Map No. 12 (Miura hantō, 三浦半島), New Series No. 28.

Walking time: About 3 hours 40 minutes.

Points of interest: Broad-leaved evergreen forest with cherry trees and wildflowers, especially attractive in spring.

GETTING THERE

The most direct means is by a Keihin Kyūkō Line (京浜急行線) express (*kyūkō*, 急行) from Shinagawa Station to Shin-Zushi (新逗子) Station. Shin-Zushi is actually the terminus of a small branch line called the Zushi Line (逗子線), which leaves the main tracks at Kanazawa-Hakkei (金沢八景) Station. Since most trains from Shinagawa follow the main line, make sure that your train is bound for Shin-Zushi, or else you have to change trains. In this case, take a faster limited express (*tokkyū*, 特急) or the still faster and more comfortable rapid limited express (*kaisoku tokkyū*, 快速特急) and transfer at Kanazawa-Bunko (金沢文庫) Station to the local train for Shin-Zushi. This can leave from either side of the platform.

A direct express to Shin-Zushi takes about 65 minutes, while the two legs of the alternative require about 35 minutes for the rapid limited express and 10 minutes for the local train. The fare in either case is ¥510.

From Shin-Zushi Station to Mt. Futago (1 hour and 50 minutes)

Leave Shin-Zushi Station by the south exit, which is nearest the front of the train as you arrive, and take the small path that lies almost straight ahead as you come out of the station. To the start of the walking path from here takes 30 minutes of skirting main roads and zigzagging through rural lanes.

About 100 meters from the station, after passing a bus yard on the right, turn right and proceed to the pedestrian crossing and traffic lights at the main road. Turn left at the lights and go along the main road for several hundred meters, passing over a river and through another set of lights and a tunnel. About 150 meters past the end of the tunnel, a small lane with a sign saying "School Road" (学路) veers off to the left. This merges with a minor road after 50 meters, and after about 10 minutes, past the shrine on the left, it meets a large road at a set of traffic lights.

Cross this intersection and almost immediately, at a traffic mirror, turn right down another lane. Just over the bridge, the road forks. Go left onto the small bitumen lane, and then left again at the fork with an overhead light and a stone wall that has an anodized bronze fence on top. This lane soon meets a larger dirt road running next to the river. Turn right and follow this road through a rural area with many cherry trees. In 10 minutes you reach a barrier to prevent access by cars and motorbikes. This road is the start of a walking path through one of the prettiest areas near Tokyo.

The path meanders gently through the hills surrounding Mt. Futago and is easy to follow at first because it is wide and there are few alternatives. A sparkling stream and an abundance of wildflowers in spring make this trail especially attractive. Some flowers common here are: *tsubaki* (camellia), white *momijiichigo* (a kind of raspberry with amber-colored fruit), purple and mauve *sumire* and *tachitsubo-sumire* (violets), and tiny mauve *sagigoke* (*Mazus miquelii* form. *albiflorus*). The tree known as *kibushi* (*Stachyurus praecox*), which has long "strings" of yellow flowers, and a large number of ferns are also found here.

About 10–15 minutes after passing the barrier, ignore the smaller path leading to the right at the handrail made of tubing and continue for about 30 minutes until you reach a signposted junction. The main path to the right becomes quite overgrown just past here, so take the left-hand route marked "usual route to Mt. Futago" (二子山順路), following the left-hand tributary of the stream that also divides here. The trail enters the stream bed and is quite steep but very picturesque. As you get higher, the water dwindles to a trickle and eventually you come to the spring that is its source.

The ensuing intersection is about 20 minutes farther on. The route for the next stage is to the right, indicated on the signpost as "the direction for Numama" (沼間方面). A recommended lunch

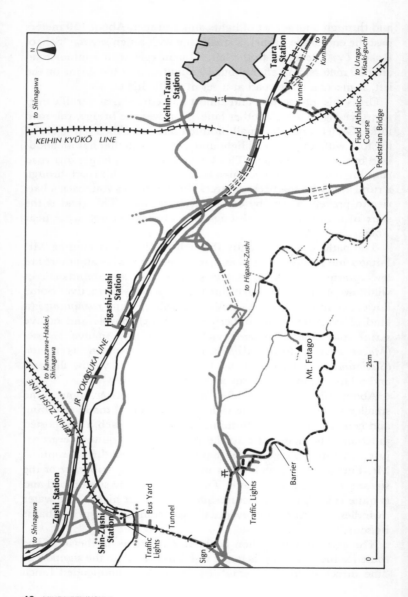

Shintō shrine on the way to Mt. Futago.

spot is, however, reached by taking the path to the left marked "to
Mt. Futago Upper Peak" (至る二子山頂上), leading to the top of Mt.
Futago (*Futagoyama*, 二子山). (The wide path to the right on the way
up returns to the main road that you crossed as you walked from
Shin-Zushi Station.) After 10 minutes you reach a clearing
suitable for lunch a few minutes before the 208-meter-high summit. Until the observation tower is rebuilt the view will be
restricted due to the height of the surrounding forest.

From Mt. Futago to Taura Station (1 hour 50 minutes)

Return to the signposted junction and walk in the direction of
Numama. This route follows ridges straddling hills covered with
the flora native to the Kantō Plain, the most attractive of which,
especially in spring, is the *yamazakura*, or wild cherry, whose
blossoms are mostly white in this area. The forest is quite dense
here, but a little farther on there are panoramic views of hills that
are wonderful when covered in spring blossoms.

After 15–20 minutes, you come to a cluster of five signs, including a fire hazard warning and a wildlife protection area
notice. While the main path to the left goes to Higashi-Zushi (東逗
子), our route is to the right, along the small path, to Taura (田浦).
This track forks almost immediately, so again go right for Taura.

After 10 minutes, there is a junction with a small sign hanging from a tree. Go left for Taura (the right-hand destination is not marked). From there until the next major junction, stay on the main path and avoid the many small unsignposted trails as you pass through *sugi* (cedar) plantations.

About 15 minutes along this path is a major, although badly marked, junction from which a divided highway can be seen through the tree branches. Turn right here in the direction the hanging yellow plastic sign indicates is for Mt. Hatake (畠山). The trail immediately splits into two, and you may take either one since the two trails soon rejoin. Then stay on the main path. When it emerges from under the tree canopy, it undulates over low ridges, with good views of the forest to the right and of the sea and harbor near Taura to the left. At some point you will catch sight of a pedestrian bridge crossing the highway. This you will have to cross, though it is hidden from view as you get closer.

The turnoff for the pedestrian bridge comes about 20 minutes after the previous main junction and is unmarked. The track to take goes steeply downhill and appears to descend to the bottom of the deep valley below and to the left. In fact, it follows a small lower ridge in the middle of this valley, so if you find you are faced with an alternative, take the upper, left-hand trail. In 15 minutes you reach the pedestrian bridge and a few minutes later, on the other side of the highway, you have a choice of paths. From here to Taura Station (田浦駅) on the JR Yokosuka Line (横須賀線) takes about 30 minutes.

Go right, down the steps past the big signs and alongside the "field athletics" course. If you have any energy left, try doing the course in reverse—it's much harder! Continue past the athletics course office, which is slightly uphill, and follow the concrete steps without turning off them all the way down to the small road at the bottom of the hill. Turn left and keep walking until a T-junction forces you to make a choice. Go right, and you soon reach the main road. Turn right again and pass through the first tunnel. Taura Station is down the street to your left.

The fare to Shinagawa is ¥760, and the journey takes just over 1 hour. Some trains stop two stations down the line at Zushi; if yours does, transfer to a train on the opposite side of the platform.

TANZAWA

Rugged peaks separated by deep forested valleys characterize Kanagawa Prefecture's Tanzawa area. The walks described here cover parts of Tanzawa–Ōyama National Park and Omote-Tanzawa Prefectural Forest, southwest of Tokyo, and provide the chance to experience beautiful mixed native forest. Tanzawa is best reached by the Odakyū Line from Shinjuku, although access to some areas is also possible via the JR Gotemba Line.

5. NIHONSUGI PASS ———————— M

Course: Shin-Matsuda Station (by bus) → Hosokawabashi → Nihonsugi Pass → Chidori Bridge → Asase-iriguchi (by bus) → Shin-Matsuda Station

Reference map: Nitchi Map No. 5 (Tanzawa sankai, 丹沢山塊), New series No. 24; or Shōbunsha Map No. 19 (Tanzawa, 丹沢), New Series No. 21.

Walking time: About 4 hours.

Points of interest: Rugged highlands with cedar and mixed forests, wildflowers, and good views of Lake Tanzawa.

GETTING THERE

From Shinjuku Station, take an Odakyū Line (小田急線) express (*kyūkō*, 急行) from Platform 4 or 5 to Shin-Matsuda (新松田) Station. As this line branches at Sagami-Ōno (相模大野) Station, make sure you are on a train bound for Odawara (小田原) or Hakone-Yumoto (箱根湯本) and *not* Enoshima (江ノ島). Some trains divide at Sagami-Ōno, so that the front and rear have different destinations. In this case, get in one of the front carriages. The trip takes 1 hour 15–35 minutes and costs ¥550.

A slightly faster (about 1 hour 5 minutes) but much more comfortable way of reaching Shin-Matsuda is to take the limited ex-

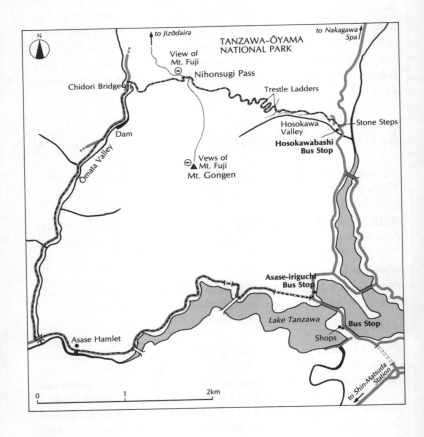

to Jizōdaira

TANZAWA–ŌYAMA
NATIONAL PARK

to Nakagawa Spa

View of Mt. Fuji

Nihonsugi Pass

Chidori Bridge

Trestle Ladders

Hosokawa Valley

Stone Steps

Dam

Hosokawabashi Bus Stop

Omata Valley

Vews of Mt. Fuji
Mt. Gongen

Asase-iriguchi Bus Stop

Lake Tanzawa

Bus Stop

Asase Hamlet

Shops

to Shin-Matsuda Station

0   1   2km

press (特急) called the "Romance Car" from Platform 2 or 3 on the same line. Note, however, that this train is less frequent, often requires booking in advance, and costs an additional ¥410.

At Shin-Matsuda Station, leave by the only exit, turn to the left, and walk a few meters to Bus Stand No. 2. There catch a No. 61, 62, 63, or 64 Fuji Kyūkō bus bound for Nakagawa Spa (*Nakagawa onsen*, 中川温泉) or Nishi-Tanzawa (西丹沢). You can get a ticket from the machine near the bus company office. Get off after 50–60 minutes at Hosokawabashi (細川橋) Bus Stop. The fare is ¥800.

From Hosokawabashi to Nihonsugi Pass (1 hour 10 minutes)

Walk for 100 meters in the direction the bus was going to the stone steps leading uphill on the left side of the road. A signpost here confirms that this is the way to Jizōdaira (地蔵平) and Nihonsugi Pass (*Nihonsugi-toge*, 二本杉峠). Climb these steps past some plots of *daikon* (Japanese giant radish) and tea bushes to a concrete road. The steps continue at the left-hand edge of the road, although they are a little overgrown. Climb these and another sign at the top directs you along a dirt path to a junction about 50 meters away. There yet another sign shows you should go right. Between spring and autumn various types of daisy and thistle bloom in this area.

From here on, there are few signs until you reach Nihonsugi Pass. Initially the trail makes its way uphill through mixed forest along the edge of the Hosokawa Valley and high above a small stream. The path becomes quite rocky and crosses several rotting "bridges" or supports, which should be negotiated carefully.

About 20 minutes from the start of the walk, be sure not to take the minor path that leads off to the left. This part of the Tanzawa–Ōyama National Park has many wildflowers, including, in the autumn, the brushlike mauve *naginatakōju* (*Elsholtzia ciliata*) and the red-beaded *mizuhiki*, a knotweed named after the ornamental paper cord used in Japan for tying presents. The trail then enters a cedar plantation where the lack of undergrowth makes the path a little difficult to make out. After 10 or so minutes, beyond a small tea plantation on the right, small unsignposted paths branch off to the left. Ignore these and stay on the main trail.

Within 5 minutes the path crosses a small stream bed from the right bank to the left, as you face uphill, and soon after you come to a T-junction. Go right, and the track will soon cross back to the other side of the bed.

After you leave the cedar plantation, you soon come to an orange trestle ladder straddling a fence enclosing a plantation of cedar saplings. Climb over and follow the path as it zigzags up the slope. At the top are good views and suitable spots for resting or having lunch. The trail to Nihonsugi Pass continues uphill to the left, over another ladder into more cedar and mixed forests, with plentiful ferns, *sasa* (dwarf bamboo), and *rindō* (gentian). There are also several old circular stone-walled pits here. The slope is steep and eroded, so tread carefully along this section.

About 30 minutes from the second ladder, you reach the 740-meter-high Nihonsugi Pass—which literally means the "Pass with Two Cedar Trees"—clearly indicated by a large sign. Here a signpost indicates the directions of several trails.

Nihonsugi Pass is also known as Fujimi Pass. Despite its name, which means the "Pass from which Mt. Fuji Can Be Seen," you will not be able to see much because of the height of the surrounding trees. For a good view of the famous cone-shaped peak, either walk for about 5 to 10 minutes along the track slightly to the right in the direction of Jizōdaira (地蔵平), or climb Mt. Gongen (権現山), which is 1,019 meters high, by ascending the path to the left for about 40 minutes. (Note that these times are not included in the time summaries for this walk).

From Nihonsugi Pass to Asase-iriguchi (2 hours 50 minutes)

From Nihonsugi Pass, follow the path straight ahead downhill marked Chidori Bridge (*Chidoribashi*, 千鳥橋). This trail is overgrown, rocky, and at times slippery, with steep drops to the left in places, so care should be taken. Also, trees felled by heavy snowfalls sometimes block the path. This route passes through more mixed forest with many vines and mushrooms, and it is quite pretty, with fine views of the Ōmata Valley. The *akebi* (Asiatic vines valued for their oily seeds and edible fruit and also as a material for basket-weaving) common along the side of the trail bear fruit late in the year. Again you will have to pass over some makeshift bridges.

Lake Tanzawa's mountain backdrop.

After reaching the bottom of the slope, you pass through long grass and soon meet a dirt road next to a logging plant. The logs are brought here from the surrounding forests by means of overhead cables. Turn left onto the road and cross Chidori Bridge. The descent from Nihonsugi Pass to this bridge takes about 40 minutes.

From Chidori Bridge, continue along the dirt road, following the river downstream through the Ōmata Valley, past a small dam and over several bridges that cross minor tributaries, some with attractive waterfalls. When the road forks, take the lower, left-hand alternative nearer the river. The banks of the river are flanked with *susuki* (Japanese pampas grass), and the dry part of the riverbed makes a good place for a rest.

One hour 20–30 minutes from Chidori Bridge, turn left at the T-junction and immediately cross a bridge. After 5–10 minutes, you go through a gate and enter a small hamlet called Asase (浅瀬). Keep walking along the road, which is now surfaced, following it along the edge of Lake Tanzawa, past several turn-offs and through several tunnels. To the left you should see a number of waterfalls with large drops, and ducks are common on the lake to the right.

About 45 minutes after leaving Asase, you emerge from a long tunnel at a T-junction. Asase-iriguchi Bus Stop is on the other side of the road, to the left. Catch any bus back to Shin-Matsuda Station (¥720), or if you have a long wait, walk across the steel suspension bridge to Tanzawa-ko Bus Stop, which takes about 10 minutes, where there are souvenir shops, coffee shops, and restaurants. From Shin-Matsuda, return via the Odakyū Line to Shinjuku Station.

6. LAKE TANZAWA TO YAGA ——— M

Course: Shin-Matsuda Station (by bus) → Kaminawa Tunnel (at Lake Tanzawa) → Mt. Ōno → Yaga Station

Reference map: Nitchi Map No. 5 (Tanzawa sankai, 丹沢山塊), New Series No. 24; or Shōbunsha Map No. 19 (Tanzawa, 丹沢), New Series No. 21.

Walking time: About 3 hours 45 minutes.

Points of interest: Varied scenery included rugged forested highlands and deep valleys, superb views of Mt. Fuji and Lake Tanzawa, open farmland, wildflowers from spring to autumn, and edible and medicinal plants.

GETTING THERE

From Shinjuku Station, take an Odakyū Line (小田急線) express (kyūkō, 急行) from Platform 4 or 5 to Shin-Matsuda (新松田) Station. As this line branches at Sagami-Ōno (相模大野) Station, make sure you are on a train bound for Odawara (小田原) or Hakone-Yumoto (箱根湯本) and *not* Enoshima (江ノ島). Some trains divide at Sagami-Ōno, so that the front and rear have different destinations. In this case, get in one of the front carriages. The trip takes 1 hour 15–35 minutes and costs ¥550.

A slightly faster (about 1 hour 5 minutes) but much more comfortable way of reaching Shin-Matsuda is to take the limited express (特急) called the "Romance Car" from Platform 2 or 3 on the same line. Note, however, that this train is less frequent, often requires booking in advance, and costs an additional ¥410.

At Shin-Matsuda Station, leave by the only exit, turn to the left and walk a few meters to Bus Stand No. 2. There catch a No. 62 or 64 Fuji Kyūkō bus bound for Nishi-Tanzawa (西丹沢) or Nakagawa Spa (*Nakagawa onsen*, 中川温泉) via Kurōkura (玄倉). The fare is ¥710 and a ticket can be bought from the machine next to the bus company office. Get off after about 40 minutes at Kaminawa Tunnel (*Kaminawa tonneru*, 神縄トンネル). Make sure you don't get off at the stop before, the name of which sounds similar; the correct stop is just after a couple of tunnels and is right next to Lake Tanzawa.

From Lake Tanzawa to Mt. Ōno (2 hours 15 minutes)

From the bus stop, walk about 60 meters back down the road in the opposite direction to that of the bus. On the left, just after passing some concrete steps and before a tunnel, is a small uphill path next to a sign indicating the direction of Miho Dam (三保ダム) and Mt. Ōno (大野山). The route from here to Mt. Ōno consists of a steep climb followed by a walk across a series of ridges.

Go up the small path and within 5 minutes you reach a junction where you turn left to Mt. Ōno, as indicated by the sign, and start to climb, taking advantage of the ropes and chains provided. Ignore the turnoff to Kaminawa (神縄) some 15 minutes later and continue straight. The climb takes you through cedar and mixed forests with a few clearings, and near the top you have good views of Lake Tanzawa and Miho Dam behind you. Provided the cloud cover is not too great, Mt. Fuji will be visible above to the left of the lake. In late summer and early autumn, some of the common flowers are large white-and-gold daisies, small mauve and yellow *yomena* (aster or starwort, the young plants of which are edible), purple *taiazami* (thistle), yellow *hahakogusa* (cottonweed), and pink-beaded *inutade* (knotgrass).

Just after a particularly steep section provided with ropes some 30–40 minutes past the trail to Kaminawa, you reach a line of ridges. A sign at this point indicates that Mt. Ōno lies 3.9 kilometers to the right. The walk from here is very pleasant, as the path wanders up and down the peaks, sometimes through thick forest and at other times overlooking cleared slopes that afford

Lake Tanzawa and Miho Dam.

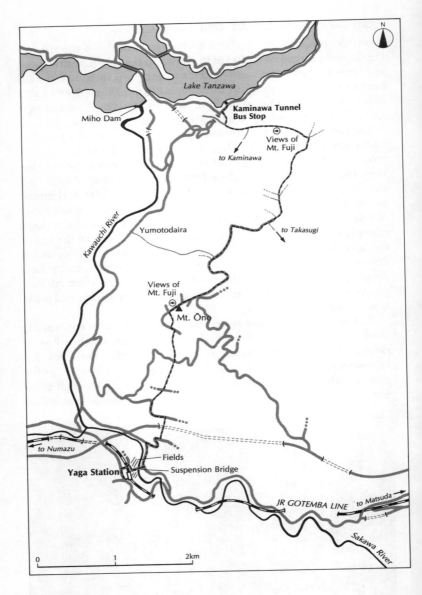

Lake Tanzawa

Kaminawa Tunnel
Bus Stop

Miho Dam

Views of
Mt. Fuji

to Kaminawa

Kawauchi River

Yumotodaira

to Takasugi

Views of
Mt. Fuji

Mt. Ōno

to Numazu

Fields

Yaga Station

Suspension Bridge

JR GOTEMBA LINE to Matsuda

Sakawa River

0   1   2km

good views of the lake and the Tanzawa Range. Some of the peaks are good lunch spots as they have small clearings. They also have boards with maps showing the part of the lake visible from that point. Many wildflowers and berry-bearing bushes and trees flourish in the surrounding forests, including, in spring and summer, *hebiichigo* (wild Indian strawberry), which has small yellow flowers, *utsugi* (deutzia), with white blossoms, and *tosamurasaki* (*Callicarpa shikokiana*, small white Japanese beauty-berries); and, in later summer and early autumn, *tsuriganeninjin* (an adenophora with white-mauve bell-like flowers, edible shoots, and medicinal roots), *komenamomi* (tiny yellow *Siegesbeckia glabrescens* flowers with green radial spokes in a star shape), *naginatakōju* (halberd-shaped purple *Elsholtzia ciliata* "sheaths"), and *yamazeri* (wild dropwort or Japanese parsley with small white "beads").

Several paths join the trail along this section, but keep to the main path and follow the signs for Mt. Ōno. After 30–40 minutes the path becomes a dirt road. Edible mountain vegetables, such as *mitsuba* (stone parsley), often used for tempura and in soup, can be found beside the road. What could be nicer than cooking wild vegetables found on your walk!

Down this road 5–10 minutes a small path not easily seen from the road leads off to the left to Takasugi (高杉), which is a tiny village perched on a mountain spur. Wild boar meat is sold in this village, where they also breed dogs. If you have time you might consider taking this detour down to Takasugi, as it is very pretty, if a little steep in places. It takes about 40 minutes to reach the village and, since it is uphill, about 1 hour to come back by the same path to the main trail. Note that these times are not included in the totals listed for this section or for the walk as a whole.

If you don't make the detour, or after you have returned to the main route after the detour, continue along the dirt road to Mt. Ōno past a turnoff to Yumotodaira (湯本平) and a camp site with huts, and an unmarked junction, after which the road surface changes to bitumen. Some 30–40 minutes from the junction with the detour to Takasugi is a four-way intersection with a very large board showing the surrounding points of interest and some hiking routes. Nearby are farms that raise cattle and grow the fodder to feed them.

The summit of Mt. Ōno (*Ōnoyama*, 大野山) is only a few minutes away, straight ahead up the concrete road past the car boom gate—ignore the dirt road leading to the left and, a little later, another road to the right. Relaxing in the rest shelter on the summit, which is 723 meters high, you have one of the best possible views of Mt. Fuji, with nearly all its famous outline visible. Below to the right, you can still see Lake Tanzawa and Miho Dam. Incidentally this area is popular as a place to collect *ōbako*, a medicinal herb used to cure a variety of complaints, particularly stomach and other alimentary disorders. The whole plant, which is gathered in spring, is boiled for this purpose, and the flowers alone are sometimes fried tempura-style as a delicacy.

From Mt. Ōno to Yaga (1 hour 30 minutes)

Continue along the bitumen road past the rest shelter and down the other side of Mt. Ōno. After about 5 minutes you come to a junction with roads to the right and straight ahead and a small path—our route—to the left to Yaga (谷峨), indicated by a sign. In places this track is quite narrow and it descends steeply, which makes it slippery even when the soil is dry. However it offers superb views of the slopes of surrounding valleys, which are covered with tea bushes, and depending on the season there may be many kinds of wildflowers.

After 5–10 minutes, this path meets a concrete road. Go downhill to the left along this road for about 20 meters where you will see the signposted continuation of the path to the right. In early summer, *hirugao* (convolvulus), *harujion* (white daisy), *noazami* (a type of thistle), and mauve clover dot this hillside. Part of the path skirts a cow yard.

Some 25 minutes from the concrete road, the track cuts across a dirt road, and within 10 minutes, just beyond a bamboo grove, it crosses a second dirt road near a tea plantation and some thatched houses. A few minutes later, near another tea plantation and some more houses, the path comes out on a bitumen road. Turn left and walk along the road. Immediately below to the right are some graves in the center of a tea plantation. Similar plantations cover the slope on the other side of the valley.

A signposted concrete path leads off to the right 5 minutes fur-

Tea plantations near Yaga.

ther along the road. Take this path and, ignoring any turnoffs, follow it for about 15 minutes, past more plantations to another bitumen road. A large divided highway bridge that spans the valley is visible from this point, which is about 20 minutes from Yaga Station. In June and July *ajisai* (hydrangea) is common here. Turn right and follow the road down to the river, then turn left, which will lead you past a weir to a blue suspension bridge over the Sakawa River.

Cross this bridge and continue along the dirt road between rice and vegetable fields. Yaga Station (谷峨駅), which is on the JR Gotemba Line (御殿場線), lies ahead to the left. To enter the station, cross the overhead bridge to your right or take the dirt path ahead that leads up to the right, cross the tracks, and take the concrete path up to the road. Walk to the left down the road to the station, crossing the tracks again to get on the correct side for the journey back to Tokyo.

The best and cheapest way to return to Shinjuku Station is to take the train to Matsuda (松田) Station (12 minutes, ¥190) and then transfer, by walking across the road to Shin-Matsuda Station, to an Odakyū Line express. However, it is also possible to continue on the Gotemba Line to Kōzu (国府津) Station and transfer to the Tōkaidō Main Line (東海道本線), which runs to Shinagawa Station (total fare ¥1,590).

7. OMOTE-TANZAWA FOREST ——— M

Course: Shibusawa Station (by bus) → Ōkura → Omote-Tanzawa Forest → Ōkura (by bus) → Shibusawa Station

Reference map: Hatano (秦野) and Ōyama (大山) 1:25,000 Sheet Maps.

Walking time: This depends on the course selected, but the total for the suggested walk is about 4 hours 20 minutes.

Points of interest: Various kinds of forest, Kokuryū Waterfall, mountain streams, wildflowers (particularly in spring and summer), butterflies, and aromatic and medicinal plants and fungi.

GETTING THERE

From Shinjuku Station, take an Odakyū Line (小田急線) express (*kyūkō*, 急行) from Platform 4 or 5 to Shibusawa (渋沢) Station. As this line branches at Sagami-Ōno (相模大野) Station, make sure you are on a train bound for Odawara (小田原) or Hakone-Yumoto (箱根湯本) and *not* Enoshima (江ノ島). Some trains divide at Sagami-Ōno, so that the front and rear have different destinations. In this case, get in one of the front carriages. The trip takes 1 hour 10–25 minutes and costs ¥490.

Leave the central exit (on the same side as you alight) of Shibusawa Station, turn right, and walk a few meters to the bus stand, where you catch a No. 2 bus bound for Ōkura (大倉), which is also your destination. This short (15 minutes) but enjoyable trip takes you past nurseries and fields. The fare is ¥160.

From Ōkura to Omote-Tanzawa Forest (1 hour)

Walk straight ahead uphill in the direction the bus was traveling and after about 20 meters turn left down the small paved road. A multitude of signs, including one for the Prefectural Forest (*Kenmin no mori*, 県民の森), point in this direction. In late spring and early summer, common along this road are the white flowers of *yukinoshita* (strawberry geranium) and *dokudami* (*Houttuynia cordata*), which is a herb whose leaves are used for stomach ailments after being dried and boiled to a concentrate. In early autumn, scarlet *higanbana* (cluster amaryllis) grows on the edges of the fields. The name *"higanbana"* is both a reference to "the other side of the river," where, according to Buddhism, souls go after death, and to the autumnal equinox, when respects are paid to ancestors and when this flower blooms.

Some 10 minutes later, just before a bend in the road, take a small signposted paved lane to the left. This lane eventually becomes a forest path (with wild strawberries beside it in late spring and summer), which after 10–12 minutes meets a concrete road at a T-junction. Turn right here, in the direction of Omote-Tanzawa Prefectural Park (*Omote-Tanzawa Kenmin no mori*, 表丹沢県民の森). The road passes a large sign announcing, in both English and Japanese, Ōyama Quasi-National Park. Large, attractive butterflies are common along this road and throughout the park. In late summer and early autumn, small blue *tsuyukusa* (dayflower or spiderwort) and long strands of *mizuhiki* (a kind of knotweed with small red petals, named after the decorative strings used for tying gifts) and *kinmizuhiki* (small yellow agrimony flowers, also named after the decorative strings) are found here as well.

About 35 minutes after turning right you come to a large map board on the left showing the boundaries of the park and its rivers and roads, and a series of paths linked by numbered junctions, from which you can choose your route. In some parts of the forest, certain species of plant predominate, for example, *mizuki* (dogwood), *sasa* (dwarf bamboo), *kashiwa* (oak), and *shida* (a type of fern).

The map board is located at junction No. 1, and the walk suggested here passes through the following signposted junctions: 1, 2, 10, 11, 12, 9, 5, and back to 1. Whatever route you choose, you should finally return to junction No. 1 in order to go back to the bus stop at Ōkura.

Suggested Walk (2 hours 30 minutes)

Go down the steps next to the map board into the small valley. Some 8 minutes after leaving this board, the path forks. Go left and after a few meters you will be confronted with the spectacular sight of Kokuryū Waterfall (黒龍の滝). This is a pleasant place to spend a while, and when you are ready to leave, go back to the

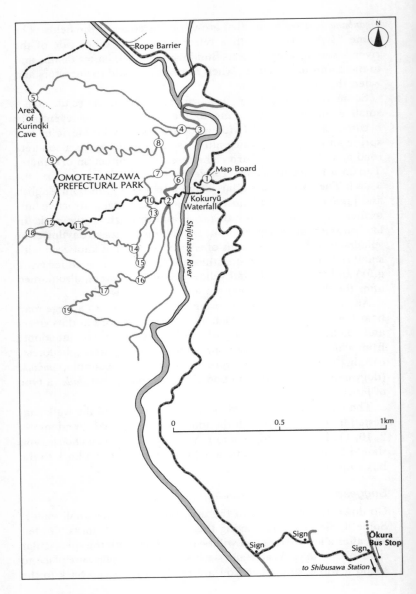

Kokuryū Waterfall.

fork and this time take the other path that follows the small stream flowing from the waterfall to the Shijūhasse River (四十八瀬川, meaning the "River with Forty-eight Rapids"), a few minutes away. The banks of this river, with their pleasant grassy areas and huge boulders jutting out into clear water a little upstream, offer one of the most attractive picnic places near Tokyo.

When you leave this spot, return to the path and cross the river by means of the makeshift bridge of logs nailed and tied together. From here, a steep climb among cedars and up fern-covered slopes leads you past picnic clearings and over a dirt road to junction No. 2. Continue uphill past more picnic sites to junction No. 10. From the river to this point takes about 20 minutes. Next head up and left to junction No. 11, then right to junction No. 12; these two sections require about 35 minutes of hard climbing.

At junction No. 12, turn right and follow the path along the top of the ridge that marks the western boundary of the prefectural forest. After about 15 minutes you reach junction No. 9. On this section the going is much easier, and occasionally there are good views to the left. Sometimes I have seen remnants of antlers around here, a sign of the wild deer in the area. Around these ridges, too, are found *sansho* (Japanese pepper), an aromatic plant used in cooking, and, in summer, *koajisai*, a type of hydrangea with clusters of small mauve flowers, and *momijiichigo*, a maple-leafed variety of wild raspberry that bears sweet amber-colored fruit.

From junction No. 9, keep walking in the same direction for another 10 minutes until you come to junction No. 5, located on a 908-meter-high peak. Near here is Kurinoki Cave (栗ノ木洞).

To return to junction No. 1, and eventually Ōkura, go straight ahead. The path soon curves to the right and begins to descend steeply, following the northern boundary of the forest. Fungi valued for their medicinal properties are found in this area. After 20 minutes, turn right on a narrow ridge, toward Ōkura (大倉). The steep descent continues and involves crossing a series of rickety wooden bridges that should be negotiated with care, one person at a time. Ignore the track that joins the main path from the left, and continue in the same direction, at times walking in the stream bed. After 20 minutes you reach a larger stream whose shady banks offer a pleasant place to rest. Note the unusual "swing," consisting of a tree root protruding from a bank undercut by erosion.

Continue by following the dirt road on the opposite side of the river downstream. After 5 minutes you may come to a sign strung across the road indicating it is closed, leaving a choice of taking the uphill path to the left, which eventually rejoins this road, or of continuing along the road past the barrier. The latter route actually presents no problems for people on foot, and it is recommended as it is more attractive. The road passes close to the river, which drops over a series of walls, gradually becoming stronger as the various tributaries converge. At one section the road narrows to a small path. Some places near the river here are excellent secluded camping sites. The path crosses a denuded slope where a landslide has blocked the road (the reason for the road being closed to vehicles). Keep following the road downhill, ignoring the road that joins from the right, and in about 40 minutes you will be back at the map board at junction No. 1.

To return to the bus stop at Ōkura, follow the route described in the "From Ōkura to Omote-Tanzawa Forest" section in reverse, which takes about 50 minutes.

8. MT. MITSUMINE ———————————— D

Course: Honatsugi Station (by bus) → Susugaya → Mt. Mitsumine → Fudōji → Kōtaku-ji Spa (by bus) → Honatsugi Station

Reference map: Nitchi Map No. 5 (Tanzawa sankai, 丹沢山塊), New Series No. 24; or Shōbunsha Map No. 19 (Tanzawa, 丹沢), New Series No. 21.

Walking time: About 4 hours 30 minutes.

Points of interest: Rugged highlands with superb mountain views, wildflowers (especially in spring), Kōtaku-ji Spa.

GETTING THERE

From Shinjuku Station, take an Odakyū Line (小田急線) express (*kyūkō*, 急行) from Platform 4 or 5 to Honatsugi (本厚木) Station. As the Odakyū Line branches at Sagami-Ōno (相模大野) Station, make sure you are on a train bound for Odawara (小田原) or Hakone-Yumoto (箱根湯本) and *not* Enoshima (江ノ島). Some trains divide at Sagami-Ōno, so that the front and rear have different destinations. In this case, get in one of the front carriages. The trip takes 48–60 minutes and costs ¥370.

A slightly faster (40–45 minutes) and much more comfortable way of getting to Honatsugi is to take the limited express (*tokkyū*, 特急) called the "Romance Car" from Platform 2 or 3 of the same line. Note, however, that this train is less frequent, often requires booking in advance, and costs an additional ¥410.

Leave Honatsugi Station by the central exit, turn left, and walk out of the northern side of the station and then over the pedestrian crossing that can be seen slightly to the right. At Bus Stand No. 4, catch a No. 20 Kanagawa Chūō Kōtsū bus bound for Miyagase (宮ヶ瀬). Get off after 25–30 minutes at Susugaya (煤ヶ谷) Bus Stop. The fare is ¥400.

From Susugaya to Mt. Mitsumine (2 hours 30 minutes)

Walk in the same direction as the bus was going, cross the stream a few yards from the bus stop and turn left along the bitumen road. In a few minutes a concrete road veers off to the right. An

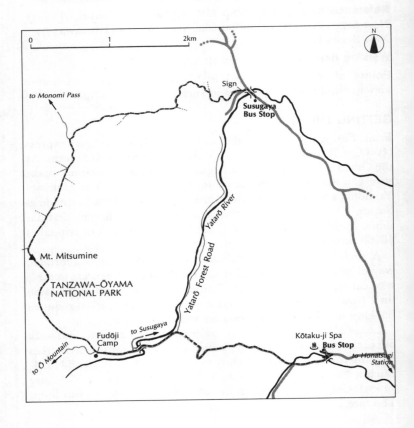

old sign here says "to the end of the Yatarō Forest Path, 1.5 km" (谷太郎林道終点, 約1.5K), and 20 meters or so further along the concrete road a newer sign announces that this is also the way to Monomi Pass (Monomi-tōge, 物見峠) and Mt. Mitsumine (Mitsumine-san, 三峰山). Go up this concrete road and continue when it becomes a small path after 100 meters.

The beginning of the path is flanked by small tea plantations on steep slopes, some of which have ingenious flying foxlike devices to bring the leaves to the road. The tea bushes soon give way to mixed forests that include hinoki (Japanese cypress) and sugi (cedar). At times the path is rocky and there are several junctions, but just follow the signs (which are all the same) to Mt. Mitsumine or stay on the main path if there is no sign.

About 50 minutes after leaving the road, the track divides at a signposted junction, with one path leading to Monomi Pass, and the other to Mt. Mitsumine and Fudōji (不動尻). At this junction there is a platform to rest on, and the view is pretty.

Continue by taking the left-hand route to Mt. Mitsumine, which takes approximately 1 hour 40 minutes of hard climbing. The path becomes progressively steeper, so it is advisable to take a few rests. After a winter with heavy snowfalls, these slopes are littered with saplings broken by the weight of the snow, giving the impression that an angry giant has trampled through the mountains. In spring, wildflowers cover sunny areas that are not sheltered by trees. Late spring flowers in this region include tsutsuji (azalea) and the white blooms of the shrubs gonzui (Euscaphis japonica), mitsubautsugi (Staphylea bumalda), and ōkamenoki (Viburnum furcatum).

Again, there are several junctions, but just follow the signs and stay on the main track. Along the way you will pass several gates and some picnic tables. Mitsumine means "Three Peaks," and after reaching the top of one peak, the path follows the ridges joining the other summits. The views are spectacular from this height, with the sides of the ridges dropping steeply away on either side of the narrow path. Ropes and chains, as well as small wooden ladder-bridges, are provided to assist you on the climb. The condition of several of the latter is suspect, so be careful when crossing them.

View near Mt. Mitsumine.

Eventually, you reach a small flat area with a wooden table and a sign indicating that you are on the summit of Mt. Mitsumine, which at 935 meters above sea level, is a scenic place to stop for lunch.

From Mt. Mitsumine to Kōtaku-ji Spa (2 hours)

The path to Kōtaku-ji Spa (*Kōtakuji onsen*, 広沢寺温泉) is a continuation of the route from Susugaya to Mt. Mitsumine, and passes through Fudōji (不動尻). Follow the path down the other side of Mt. Mitsumine in the direction marked Fudōji. This track is steep and slippery in wet weather and has many small wooden bridges, some made of logs bound together, that crisscross over a small stream. This stream, which first appears about 40 minutes after leaving the top of Mt. Mitsumine, flows over a series of man-made walls and through a very picturesque valley to eventually become the Yatarō River (谷太郎川).

Some 25 minutes later, you pass by a path to sacred Ō Mountain (Ōyama, 大山). Continue past a camp site with some buildings at Fudōji, then go straight ahead along the gravel and concrete path that runs over the river and into the car park. (Just before crossing the river, a path leads off to the left. Although this route is not described here, it is possible to take this path, which follows the river, back to Susugaya, near where you got off the bus. This would take about 1 hour 10 minutes.)

Walk through the car park and down the bitumen and concrete road. This takes you through a tunnel and past some fields and fish-breeding ponds to your left and a road to a forest in the Ozawa area to your right. About 50 minutes from Fudōji, immediately after crossing a bridge, turn hard left up a dirt road at a corner where there is a small Buddha and some stone tablets. Some 100 meters ahead are a group of buildings, comprising Kōtaku-ji Spa and Kōtaku Temple, and a bus stop.

The buses from Kōtaku-ji Spa are not frequent, so if you have a long wait there is no better excuse for taking a dip in that soothing mountain water and relaxing those aching muscles. The cost for the first hour is ¥1,000 per person for a private room and a dip (plus ¥100 if you don't bring your own towel), and ¥500 for each subsequent hour. It is advisable to make a reservation, by telephoning (0462)48-0011.

The bus journey back to Honatsugi Station (the stop there is known as *Honatsugi-eki-mae*) costs ¥310 and takes about 35 minutes. You may have to transfer after about 10 minutes, since this bus is used mostly to shuttle people to a stop on the main bus route outside a rehabilitation center. Simply get off with everyone else and wait for the next bus—you don't pay until you get off the second bus. If you don't wish to wait for the bus at Kōtaku-ji Spa, walk down the bitumen road you turned off for a further 15 minutes to the main road and take a bus from there.

From Honatsugi Station, catch an express or limited express on the Odakyū Line back to Shinjuku.

TAKAO AND ENVIRONS

A terrain of medium-sized mountains and small lakes that takes in parts of western Tokyo, Yamanashi Prefecture, and Kanagawa Prefecture, Takao and the districts adjacent to it are among the closest and most popular hiking areas for Tokyoites, not least because of their accessibility from the capital. Consequently, on Sundays the major trails are rather busy. It is probably best also to avoid Takao on Fridays, due to the large numbers of schoolchildren on excursions. The trails described cover parts of the Tama River and Takao National Park, together with areas lying to the west of these, and they can be easily reached by the Keiō and JR Chūō Lines from Shinjuku, and the JR Hachikō Line from Hachiōji.

9. TAMA RIVER ——————————————— E

Course: Komiya Station → Tama River → through the nearby hills to Seibu-Takiyamadai Bus Stop (by bus) → Hachiōji Station.

Reference map: Haijima (拝島) 1:25,000 Sheet Map.

Walking time: About 2 hours 30 minutes.

Points of interest: River and forest scenery, various birds and wildflowers.

GETTING THERE

From Platform 8 of JR Shinjuku Station, take a Chūō Line (中央線) rapid service train (*kaisoku*, 快速) or special rapid service train (*tokubetsu kaisoku*, 特別快速) bound for Takao (高尾) or Hachiōji (八王子) stations, and get off at Hachiōji. These trains take 51 and 39 minutes, respectively, to reach Hachiōji, where you transfer to the Hachikō Line (八高線). Trains leave about twice an hour from Platform 1. Get off after about 8 minutes at the second stop, Komiya (小宮) Station. Note that you may have to push the white button to open the doors of this diesel train. The total fare from Shinjuku is ¥640.

From Komiya Station to the Tama River (25 minutes)

This section describes the route through the streets of Komiya to the river. If you lose your way, ask someone to direct you to the the Tama River (*Tamagawa*, 多摩川) and then head west (left) until you recognize the description in the next section.

Leave Komiya Station by the only exit and take the small road that forks to the left. This road turns hard left at a set of traffic mirrors, and then hard right, before soon reaching an intersection, where there is a cultivated field on the right and a barbershop on the left. Turn left and continue straight, through an intersection and past a Meiji-period (1868–1912) storehouse on your right. A little further on, about 20 meters before a corner with a work yard and an overhead gantry crane, a lane leads to the right. Go down this and then turn left at the cemetery. Turn right at the next lane to reach the main road after a short distance. It takes 10–15 minutes to get here from the station.

Turn left and follow the small service road parallel and to the left of the main road, under the flyover and then under the railway line. You are now in an open area, where kingfishers and oriental greenfinches can often be spotted. Wildflowers common in summer include daisies, blue *tsuyukusa* (dayflower or spiderwort), pink *hirugao* (convolvulus), *yōshuyamagobō* (phytolacca) and yellow *matsuyoigusa* (oenothera). Continue along this road past a baseball field some distance on the right, some houses and cultivated fields, and a *shiitake* (mushroom) farm on the left, where you can see the rows of stacked logs for growing the mushrooms. When the road merges with another small bitumen road, turn hard right and walk down to the Tama River levee bank. There is a yellow-and-black striped steel barrier at the end of the road. From the flyover to here takes about 10 minutes.

Along the Tama River (1 hour 10 minutes)

In front to the right a low wall across the river can be seen. The resulting pool of water to the left is a popular fishing spot for both men and birds. The width of the river plain here, much of it

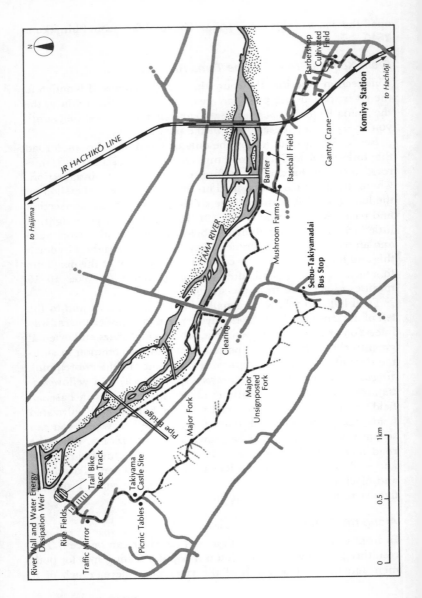

N

River Wall and Water Energy
Dissipation Weir

Traffic Mirror

Rice Fields

Trail Bike Race Track

Picnic Tables

Takiyama Castle Site

Pipe Bridge

Major Fork

Major
Unsignposted
Fork

Clearing

TAMA RIVER

JR HACHIKŌ LINE

to Haijima

Seibu-Takiyamadai
Bus Stop

Mushroom Farms

Barrier

Baseball Field

Gantry Crane

Barbershop

Cultivated
Field

Komiya Station

to Hachiōji

0   0.5   1km

covered in reeds, can be gauged by looking across at the high-rise apartment buildings near the opposite bank. Incidentally, the beauty of this area makes it a frequent choice as a location for shooting scenes for television dramas.

Walk to the left along the levee bank, past a small cow yard. This top path veers away from the river just before another mushroom farm, so climb down the stone embankment to where the southern half of the river plain becomes wider. The small path that begins here is quite stony in places. You are now faced with the following choices:

1. When there is little vegetation, in winter, it is possible to walk very close to the river. It may be a little difficult to follow the path at times but, as long as you keep going upstream, you should have no problem in completing the course. After 5 minutes or so, you cross a small rock-walled drain, after which you walk on the pebbles next to the water.

2. In late spring and summer, however, the thick vegetation makes it difficult to follow the edge of the river. In this case, use the well-defined path that leads quickly away from the river but stays on the river plain. In less than 10 minutes, turn right onto the larger path you meet. About 5 minutes later, you bear right onto a bitumen road. Among the many summer wildflowers here and along the riverside areas are tiny mauve *hekusokazura* (*Paederia scandens* var. *mairei*), pink *komatsunagi* (indigo plant), orange *yabukanzō* (tawny day lily), white roses, and small yellow *kawarasaiko* (*Potentilla chinensis*), as well as pink and white "brushes" of *nemunoki* (silk tree).

Whichever route you choose, after about 20 minutes you reach two large adjacent bridges. Pass under these. If you arrived by the small bitumen road, take the dirt path to the right, just before the first bridge. Near the river is an excellent area for birdwatching, especially for wintering ducks, or for having lunch, resting, or taking in a little nature. *Tsugumi* (dusky thrush), *hidorigamo* (wigeon), *kosogi* (little egret), *karugamo* (spot-billed duck), *magamo* (mallard), *chōgenbō* (kestrel), *aosagi* (gray heron), *kaitsuburi* (little grebe), *okayoshigamo* (gadwall), *mikoaisa* (smew), and *hamashigi* (dunlin) all frequent this part of the river.

From here, the path initially follows the river bank quite closely but gradually veers away. If you cannot find the start of the path among the reeds near the river bank, go to the clearing near the bridges at their furthest point from the river and take the well-defined path slightly to the right at the far end of the clearing. Turn right onto another large path after a few minutes. In the rainy season, you may need to ford a stream a little further on.

Stay on the wide main path and, 20–25 minutes later, you will pass under another structure, this time a pipe bridge. Another 20–25 minutes further on, not long after a wall and a sloping water energy dissipation weir stretching across the river become visible, you arrive at a fence and part of a dirt trail bike race track on the left. Cut across this track to the unsurfaced road opposite, and follow the small unpaved road located a little to the left to a bitumen road flanked with rice fields, which leads uphill.

To Seibu-Takiyamadai via the Nearby Hills (55 minutes)

Walk up the bitumen road and through the intersection with a traffic mirror, veering slightly left, in the direction indicated as for the site of Takiyama Castle (滝山城跡). Uphill are bamboo stands on both sides of the road. Ignore the road that soon leads to the left, and proceed up the concrete, then stone, road. At one bend, although there is no intersection, there are signposts on either side of the road indicating "Takiyama Municipal Park" (滝山都立公園) and "Takiyama Castle Site, Takiyama Highway" (滝山城跡, 滝山街道).

About 10 minutes later, at the top of the rise and just off to the

Sunday fishing by the Tama River.

left, is the entrance to the site of Takiyama Castle. Several boards around the site show the former locations of the main command post (本丸), the central (中の丸), secondary (二の丸), and tertiary (三の丸) quarters, and the retainers' residences (家臣屋敷) of this sixteenth-century fortress. Only modern buildings can be found there now, but it is a good place to rest, with extensive views of the Tama River plain and the surrounding valley. Opposite the castle site, on the other side of the road, are picnic tables and seats in a clearing.

Continue along the surfaced road, which is lined with *sakura* (cherry) trees. Within 100 meters, at a bend, a wide dirt path branches off straight ahead. Follow this dirt track labelled "Takiyama Hill Hiking Course" (滝山丘陵ハイキングコース). Many other paths, some large, lead off, but stay on the main trail with signs for "Takiyama Highway via Kobu Park" (古峰園地を経て滝山街道). This very pretty route meanders gently across the ridges of small heavily forested hills. Summer flowers in these hills include yellow-and-white *yamayuri* (gold-banded lily) and white *tōgibōshi* (a type of plantain lily). To the left are more views.

After about 15 minutes, again at a bend in the trail, another dirt path branches off straight ahead. At the bend, there is also a small track to the left, tables and chairs above to the right, and a concrete garbage bin base. Take the dirt path straight ahead, not the main downhill track.

At another unmarked fork 10 minutes later, bear right—a practice course of a driving school should soon be visible below on the left. A further 10 minutes of walking will bring you to an intersection with steps leading down to the left and a sign indicating National Highway No. 16 (国道16号線) in the same direction. Go down the steps, turn left onto the bitumen road, and follow it the short distance down to the main highway, where you veer left.

Cross this highway at the pedestrian lights to Seibu-Takiyamadai (西武滝山台) Bus Stop on the opposite side. Nishi-Tōkyō buses go from here to Haijima (拝島) Station and Hachiōji Station North Entrance (八王子線北口). Take the latter bus to the terminus (25 minutes, ¥270).

Return to Shinjuku by a Chūō Line rapid service train or special rapid service train from Platform 3. The fare is ¥450.

10. MT. TAKAO ——————————————— E

Course: Takao-san-guchi Station → Mt. Inari → Mt. Takao summit → Takao-san-guchi Station

Reference map: Nitchi Map No. 4 (Jimba Takao, 陣馬高尾), New Series No. 23; or Shōbunsha Map No. 20 (Takao Jimba, 高尾陣馬), New Series No. 22.

Walking time: Total for suggested walk about 2 hours 20 minutes, though there are many alternative courses.

Points of interest: Good views of surrounding mountains (including Mt. Fuji) and the Kantō Plain, magnificent colors in autumn and cherry blossoms in spring, Hiwatari Festival (early March), Yakuō Temple's Takibiraki Ceremony (early April).

GETTING THERE

From Platform 3 (occasionally Platform 2) of Shinjuku Keiō Station, take a Keiō Line (京王線) limited express (*tokkyū*, 特急) or express (*kyūkō*, 急行) to Takao-san-guchi (高尾山口) Station, the terminus of one major branch of this line. These trains take 47 and 53 minutes, respectively, and the fare is ¥340. Do not confuse Takao-san-guchi with the station before, called Takao (高尾). Note that the front and rear of some limited expresses have different destinations (Keiō-Hachiōji 京王八王子 and Takao-san-guchi). The train separates at Takahatafudō (高幡不動) Station, with the rear carriages going to Takao-san-guchi.

It is also possible to go by JR Chūō Line (中央線) to Takao Station and then transfer to the Keiō Line for the last part of the ride.

Around Takao

Emerging from the only exit of Takao-san-guchi Station, turn right and follow the lane that runs parallel to the river through the town of Takao. You soon pass by a small bridge leading to the Takao Museum of Natural History and Takao Youth Hostel. Visit the museum if you want a look at the displays of the fauna and flora of the area.

If you are walking here in March, take note that on the second Sunday the spectacular Hiwatari (fire-walking) Festival is held

Looking across Yakuō Temple to the Kantō Plain.

each year at a site next to the museum. A procession of brilliantly clad priests carrying conch shells makes its way here, fires are lit, and the priests walk barefoot on the smoldering embers. You can join in too, if you want to.

Continue past some stalls, shops, houses, and restaurants, including one called "Masutsuribori" (マスツリボリ), where customers can select fresh trout caught in a large pool and have them cooked. Another local specialty of many restaurants here is *tororosoba*, noodles served with grated mountain yams, which have a slightly "slimy" texture. When you come to the road near a bridge, veer to the right and walk in the direction of the cable car and chair lift stations, which are only about 100 meters away. From the station to here takes only 5–10 minutes.

Climbing Mt. Takao (1 hour)

There are many alternative routes up Mt. Takao (*Takao-san*, 高尾山). Most are relatively easy, well-marked paths, and if you do get lost, simply continue uphill! In addition to the many small linking tracks, there are six major trails that are assigned numbers and

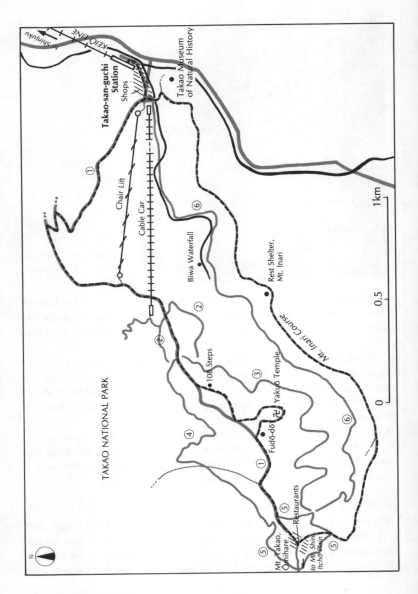

TAKAO NATIONAL PARK

Takao-san-guchi Station
Shops
KEIO LINE
to Shinjuku

Takao Museum of Natural History

Chair Lift

Cable Car

Biwa Waterfall

Rest Shelter, Mt. Inari

Mt. Inari Course

108 Steps

Yakuō Temple

Fudō-dō

Restaurants

Mt. Takao, Ōmihara

to Mt. Shiro, Itchō-daira

0   0.5   1km

N

have names. The times given here for completing the courses are the official ones given at Mt. Takao, intended for families with small children. They thus assume a slower pace compared to the times given elsewhere in this guide. The trails are: Trail 1. Nature Course (1 hour 50 minutes); Trail 2. Forest Course (30 minutes); Trail 3. Plants Course (1 hour); Trail 4. Forest and Animal Course (45 minutes); Trail 5. Man and Nature Course (30 minutes); and Trail 6. Forest and Water Course (1 hour 20 minutes). These are all marked on the map accompanying this walk. Trail 1 is in fact the road on the right leading uphill past a car park, and it traces the original path to Yakuō Temple. Trail 6 commences from beyond the left side of the cable car station. The other numbered trails branch off these two higher up.

Other ways of getting to the top are by cable car and by chair lift (to the right of the cable car). Both cost ¥420 one-way (note that the tickets are sold at different booths), and the ride up the mountain takes about 6 and 12 minutes, respectively.

For the ascent of Mt. Takao, I recommend a longer alternative to the numbered trails, since it is a wide, attractive path and is less used than the others.

To the left of the cable car station but before the start of Trail 6, a path, with a sign saying "Mt. Inari Course" (稲荷山コース), crosses a small stream and then leads up steep steps. Follow this trail, ignoring the minor tracks that branch off, as well as a larger one that heads downhill. In a few minutes, you come to a tiny shrine. Although this first part of the climb is quite steep, after 15 minutes or so the path flattens out. About 15 minutes later, at the top of a lesser peak (Mt. Inari) is a shelter with good views—a timely place for a rest!

Stay on the wide path. The many maple trees here create beautiful red and gold arches in autumn, and in April the cherry tree blossoms on some of the other paths are similarly attractive. At a point 15–20 minutes from the shelter you will be able to enjoy panoramic views of Mt. Fuji and the surrounding ranges. A path to Trail 6, marked "to Nature Study Course No. 6" (自然研究路 6 号線へ) joins from the right a few minutes later. Go straight ahead along the Mt. Inari Course toward Ōmihare (大見晴) and the summit of Mt. Takao (高尾山頂).

Some 10 minutes further, at a signposted junction with paths veering to either side, take the steps directly ahead, marked "Ōmihare, Mt. Takao summit." The left-hand path is Trail 5, which circles the summit, and that direction also leads toward nearby Mt. Shiro (城山) and Itchō Plain (一丁平). The path to the right is the continuation of Trail 5, heading toward Yakuō Temple and Biwa Waterfall.

At the top of the steps is the summit of Mt. Takao, also known as Ōmihare, where there are restaurants and picnic tables and seats. To the left, on the same side of the peak, is another branch of the path to Itchō Plain and Mt. Shiro. At the very top is a map board and a plaque indicating the direction of well-known landmarks such as Mt. Tanzawa (丹沢山), Ō Mountain (大山), Eno Island (江ノ島), Mt. Mitake (御岳山), Mt. Fuji (富士山), and Tokyo (東京).

Descending Mt. Takao (1 hour)

Go down the wide earthen steps on the other side of the peak. The path that immediately joins from the right is Trail 5 (which meets Trails 3 and 6). Trail 5 extends to the left. Passing these trails, follow the signs to Takao-san-guchi (高尾山口) along the wide dirt path.

On the way you will see several signs providing information on and pictures of the local fauna. These include details of twenty-five species of furry Japanese animal, such as *kitsune* (fox), *mogura* (mole), *saru* (monkey), *nezumi* (rat), *kōmori* (bat), *tanuki* (raccoon dog), *ten* (marten), *risu* (small squirrel), *musasabi* (giant flying squirrel), *itachi* (weasel) and *inoshishi* (wild boar). Among the 100 species of bird found locally at various times of the year are *uguisu* (bush warbler), *tsugumi* (dusky thrush), *kojukei* (bamboo partridge), *hototogisu* (little cuckoo), *shijūkara* (great tit), and *buppōsō* (broadbilled roller, which makes a sound supposedly resembling a Buddhist chant). There are also some 5,000 kinds of insect in this area. While you are unlikely to see many animals except at dusk or away from the busier areas, quite a few birds can be spotted with a sharp eye or, better still, a good pair of binoculars.

In about 10 minutes you reach a stone path that enters the rear of Fudō-dō, an inner sanctuary of Yakuō Temple (*Yakuōin*, 薬王院).

Follow the paving past Fudō-dō and down stone steps to the temple *honsha* (main shrine), which is designated a "cultural asset." This building has fine carvings on the eaves, and on the side opposite to the stone path there are some interesting smaller shrines. In one, the *inari* (a fox deity) is the dominant image, and next to this is an unusual shrine with many different *geta* (clogs). The front of the main structure is flanked by *tengu* (long-nosed goblin) figures, the one on the left being a *karasutengu* (crow-faced goblin). At the sides of the steps leading down are thirty-six bronze child icons.

Down more steps are the *hondō* (main hall) and other associated buildings of Yakuō Temple, which is reputed to have been first built in A.D. 744. Around the beginning of April each year, priests of the Shingon sect lead devotees in the ancient ritual cleansing ceremony, called "Takibiraki," in the cold water of three waterfalls around Mt. Takao.

Beyond the impressive main entrance lies a road that you should now follow. Flanked at first by many souvenir shops and then by Japanese lanterns, the road soon splits: to the left is a gently descending road, and to the right a path leading to the famous 108 steps, one for each earthly sin.

About 5–10 minutes further along, past the giant *takosugi*, a very old cedar tree with huge octopuslike roots, and the entrance to Takao Natural Park, the road divides. A few minutes away to the left is the upper cable car station (the sign at the fork gives the times of the final rides for both the cable car and the chair lift), but unless you want to take the cable car down, continue along the main road. Trail 2 veers off to the right, and after passing some more shops and a bank of powerful telescopes, you come to the chair lift station.

To complete the suggested trail, walk down the road (which is Trail 1), past the chair lift. Avoid any turnoffs, and in about 20 minutes you will be at the bottom of the mountain, next to the lower cable car and chair lift stations. Turn left just before the river, and take the small lane back to Takao-san-guchi Station for the train to Shinjuku.

11. MT. KURATAKE ——————— M

Course: Torisawa Station → Anaji Pass → Mt. Kuratake → Tateno Pass → Yanagawa Station

Reference map: Nitchi Map No. 4 (Jimba Takao, 陣馬高尾), New Series No. 23; or Shōbunsha Map No. 20 (Takao Jimba, 高尾陣馬), New Series No. 22.

Walking time: About 4 hours.

Points of interest: Deciduous forest with many birds, and good views of the Okutama and Tanzawa mountains.

GETTING THERE

From JR Shinjuku Station, take a Chūō Line (中央線) ordinary train (*futsū*, 普通), bound for Ōtsuki (大月) or Kōfu (甲府), to Torisawa (鳥沢) Station. These leave from Platforms 5, 7, or 8, depending on the time. Take care not to board the more luxurious long-distance trains, which levy a surcharge and do not stop at Torisawa.

If the departure times are inconvenient, catch a special rapid service train (*tokubetsu kaisoku*, 特別快速) or rapid service train (*kaisoku*, 快速) from Platform 8 to Tachikawa (立川), Hachiōji (八王子), or Takao (高尾) Station (trains with Takao as their destination have the most frequent connections), and transfer, since some trains that are suitable originate from here bound for Ōtsuki, Kōfu, Kobuchizawa (小淵沢), and Matsumoto (松本).

The fare from Shinjuku to Torisawa is ¥1,260, and the journey takes 1 hour 25–40 minutes (excluding connection time).

From Torisawa Station to Mt. Kuratake (2 hours 20 minutes)

Leave Torisawa Station by its only exit, turn right, and follow the small street around to the main road, where you turn right again. Walk in this direction for about 8 minutes until a small road leads off to the right. There is a sign for Mt. Takahata (高畑山) here.

Take this road across the railway line and veer left. Bear right at the T-junction a few minutes later and then keep to the right at the fork with the stone figure of Jizō, the guardian deity of children and travelers, shortly after. Stay on this road which leads

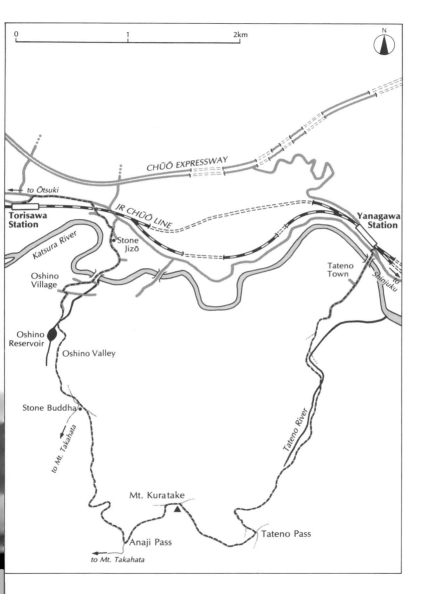

up the hill, down the other side, and across the Katsura River.

Subsequently, ignore roads leading off to the left (across another bridge) and right about 10 minutes after the stone figure. Small blue *inunofuguri* (veronica, similar to germander speedwell) flowers grow on the side of the road here in early spring. Turn left at the signposted T-junction in Oshino Village, and then right up the next lane. This soon becomes a small dirt road high above a stream. The road peters out into a path that, about 10 minutes later, skirts a greenish pond (Oshino Reservoir) surrounded by pampas grass. This trail cuts through cedar plantations and mostly deciduous native forest, and then runs parallel to the stream in Oshino Valley, with its many small falls, eventually crossing a bridge over the rocky watercourse.

Take either of the unmarked tracks at the junction about 20 minutes from the pond (they soon rejoin), but keep left, in the direction of Mt. Kuratake (倉岳山), at the stone Buddha a few minutes later. To the right lies Mt. Takahata, from where it is also possible to reach Mt. Kuratake, though I will not describe that route here. Soon after, at another stone Buddha, keep to the right.

After a very rocky section, the trail leaves the stream to ascend the slope to Anaji Pass (穴路峠). This route has been used since ancient times because of the access provided by the pass. It is particularly attractive due to the huge *akamatsu* (Japanese red pine), and springtime flowering trees and wildflowers that include some of the rose family, not to mention the many birds, such as *shijūkara* (great tit). Animals known to frequent this area include the *ten* (marten) and *musasabi* (giant flying squirrel). You should arrive at the pass after about 1 hour. There, turn left, in the direction of the summit of Mt. Kuratake (倉岳山々頂). The right-hand path goes to Mt. Takahata.

From this point the path winds across ridges and is a little arduous at times. At the small junction approximately 20 minutes further along, turn right toward Mt. Kuratake (indicated as 倉岳山頂). The 990-meter-high summit of Mt. Kuratake (*Kuratakeyama*, 倉岳山) is only a few minutes away and is an excellent spot for lunch, with outstanding views of the Okutama mountains to the north and the Tanzawa mountains to the south.

Winter walkers having lunch on the summit of Mt. Kuratake.

From Mt. Kuratake to Yanagawa Station (1 hour 40 minutes)

Make sure you take the path to the right, indicated as the direction of Tateno Pass (立野峠), down the other side of the summit. The initial descent is very steep but extremely scenic, with many Japanese pines and their characteristic high branch canopy.

In 20–25 minutes, you should come, first, to the top of a minor peak with good views of Mt. Fuji in clear weather, and, a few minutes later, to the junction at Tateno Pass (*Tateno-tōge*). Turn left toward Yanagawa Station (梁川駅), and continue past the unsignposted track to the left shortly after. The trail soon meets the Tateno River and passes a small shelter ingeniously constructed with rocks under the roots of a large tree. Various birds, among them the *uso* (bullfinch), make their home in this broad-leaved forest, which also boasts in spring of the exotic *katakuri* (dogtooth violet), as well as *sumire* (violet) and *kikeman* (corydalis) flowers of various colors. Eventually, the path traces a route high above the stream, into which flow several tributaries. A number of these are crossed by way of small bridges. Ignore any paths that lead off, and be wary of the eroded sections of the path.

About 1 hour later, the path ends at a road. Yanagawa Station is less than 15 minutes away, on the other side of the valley. Follow the road past the edge of Tateno Town and over the bridge to the main road. Cross this road and walk up the path to the station.

The fare to Shinjuku is ¥1,090. If the ticket office is unattended, obtain a ticket from the nearby machine by pushing the button, and pay for your fare on the train or at your destination. It may be necessary to transfer at Takao, Hachiōji, or Tachikawa to get to Shinjuku. The total travel time should be 1 hour 20–35 minutes.

12. THE NORTHERN TAKAO RIDGE — D

Course: Keiō-Hachiōji Station (by bus) → Jimba-kōgen-shita → Wada Pass → Mt. Jimba → Myōō Pass → Mt. Tōko → Mt. Hachiōji-shiro → Zōkei-daigaku-mae (by bus) → Takao Station

Reference map: Nitchi Map No. 4 (Jimba Takao, 陣馬高尾), New Series No. 23; or Shōbunsha Map No. 20 (Takao Jimba, 高尾陣馬), New Series No. 22.

Walking time: About 5 hours 45 minutes.

Points of interest: Spring wildflowers, good views from Mt. Jimba, a large variety of birds, historic Hachiōji Castle and the castle lookout sites.

GETTING THERE

From Platform 3 (occasionally Platform 2) of Shinjuku Keiō Station, catch a Keiō Line (京王線) limited express (*tokkyū*, 特急) or rapid service train (*kaisoku*, 快速) bound for Keiō-Hachiōji (京王八王子) and get off at the terminus. These take about 36 and 55 minutes, respectively. Be sure not to catch a train for the other major destination, Takao-san-guchi (高尾山口), unless it is one of the limited expresses that go to both places by dividing at Takahatafudō (高幡不動), in which case you should get in one of the front carriages. The fare to Keiō-Hachiōji is ¥310.

An alternative is to travel to Hachiōji (八王子) Station by the JR Chūō Line (中央線).

Directly in front of Keiō-Hachiōji Station is Bus Stand No. 1, from where you take a No. #15 bus bound for Jimba-kōgen-shita (陣馬高原下), getting off at the terminus. (The bus number must have the character 陣 in front of it, as several other buses also use this number.) The journey lasts approximately 55 minutes and costs ¥660. If you catch the Chūō Line train to JR Hachiōji Station, this bus also stops at Bus Stand No. 1 outside that station.

From Jimba-kōgen-shita to Mt. Tōko (2 hours 20 minutes)

Walk uphill from the bus stop and turn right into Jimba Avenue (*Jimba kaidō*) after a few meters. This road follows a small stream up toward the summit of Mt. Jimba.

The walk is pleasant, with many birds and spring wildflowers such as: yellow *yamabuki* (Japanese rose or globeflower), *kusanoō* (great celandine or tetterwort) and *miyamakikeman* (corydalis); white *momijiichigo* (maple-leaf raspberry), *kusaichigo* (strawberry) and tiny *tsurukanokosō* (vine valerian); small purple *kiransō* (ground pine or bugle); and mauve *murasakikeman* (another corydalis). In addition, patches of wild *sakura* (cherry) trees can be seen between and above cedar plantations to the left, and the views of the surrounding countryside open out as you climb higher.

After 45–60 minutes, you reach the clearing at Wada Pass (*Wada-tōge*, 和田峠), where there are several shops, a shelter, and a car park. Leave the road and climb the steps next to a path on the left. This is the beginning of a well-marked route that snakes through Meiji Forest and Takao National Park to Mt. Takao.

After 20–25 minutes, you arrive at a small plateau with a shop and tables and seats. You will also pass a second shop on your way to the nearby 857-meter summit of Mt. Jimba (*Jimba-san*, 陣馬山), where there are excellent 360° views and a statue of a war horse (*jimba*). You may wish to stop here for lunch.

Descend the other side of the summit, along the trail marked "Kantō Community Path, Myōō Pass 1.9 km, Mt. Kagenobu 5.7 km" (関東ふれあいの道 明王峠 1.9 km 景信山 5.7 km). The forest flanking the trail is alternately native and planted, the two sometimes coexisting on opposite sides of the path. Several signposted paths branch off the main trail to the left (to Jimba-kōgen Mountain Hut, and to Jimba-kōgen Camp) and to the right (to the JR Chūō Line's Fujino Station, via Tochiya Ridge, 藤野駅 栃谷尾根, and to Tochiya Mineral Springs and Jimba-tozan-guchi Bus Stop, 栃谷鉱泉 陣馬登山口バス停), but continue to follow signs for Myōō Pass (明王峠) and Mt. Kagenobu (景信山) along this *sasa* (dwarf bamboo)-bordered ridge.

Among the birds to be seen in these mountains are: the resident *yamadori* and *kiji* (copper and common pheasants), *kojukei* (bamboo partridge), hawks, *ikaru* (Japanese grosbeak), *onaga* (azure-winged magpie), *aogera* (Japanese green woodpecker), and *shijūkara*, *yamagara*, *enaga*, and *higara* (great, varied, long-tailed, and coal tits); in summer, *sashiba* (gray-faced buzzard-eagle), *hototogisu* (little cuckoo), dollarbirds, *sanshōkui* (ashy minivet), *kurotsugumi*

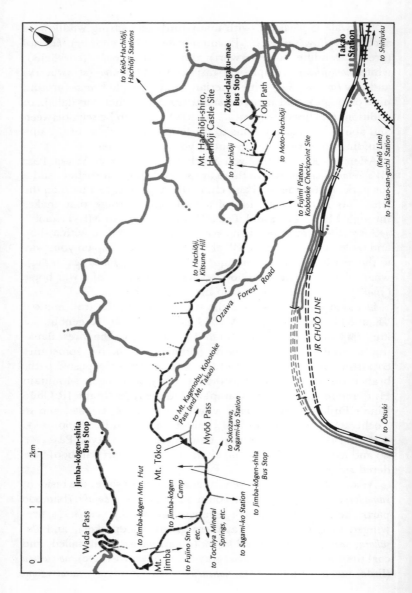

(gray thrush), *yabusame* (short-tailed bush warbler), eastern crowned warblers, and *kibitaki* and *ōruri* (narcissus and blue-and-white flycatchers); and, in winter, *misosazai* (wren), *ruribitaki* (bluetail), *jōbitaki* (daurian redstart), thrushes, *uso* (bullfinch), *shime* (hawfinch), *kikuitadaki* (goldcrest), and *aoji*, *kashiradaka*, and *kuroji* (black-faced, rustic, and gray buntings).

Some 30–40 minutes further along at Myōō Pass (*Myōō-tōge*, 明王峠) is a junction with an adjacent rest shelter. The right-hand trail leads to Sagami-ko Station (相模湖駅) on the JR Chūō Line, near Lake Sagami, so veer left toward Mt. Kagenobu and Kobotoke Pass (景信山 小仏峠). About 10 minutes later is a signposted path to the left (back to Jimba-kōgen-shita Bus Stop) and then, soon after, another to the right, to Sokozawa and Sagami-ko Station (底沢 相模湖駅). This latter path has pink *kusaboke* (small Japanese quince) wildflowers along its sides in spring. However, keep on the main path toward Mt. Kagenobu and Kobotoke Pass for about 8 minutes to where a small path diverges uphill to the left. Follow this path, marked "Hachiōji Castle Site, 8.2 km" (八王子城址 8.2 km). The wider alternative path leads to Mt. Takao via Mt. Kagenobu, Kobotoke Pass, and Mt. Shiro.

The small peak, Mt. Tōko (*Tōkoyama*, 堂所山), reached after 5 minutes, is the beginning of the Northern Takao Ridge (*Kita-Takao-san-ryō*) trail.

From Mt. Tōko to Hachiōji Castle Lookout (2 hours 35 minutes)

At the T-junction just after the summit, bear left toward "Northern Takao Ridge, Fujimi Plateau, Mt. Hachiōji-shiro" (北高尾山稜 富士見台 八王子城山). The right-hand Okutakao mountain trail (奥高尾縦走路) joins the path to Mt. Takao. This is an excellent route for viewing unusual spring flowers, among them spiky pink and mauve *ikarisō* (barrenwort) and white *hitorishizuka* (*Chloranthus japonicus*). Also, several types of the curved-top *tennanshō* (*Arisaema*) plant are common.

Stay on the main ridge trail, ignoring the small path you meet to the right after 35 minutes, which goes down to the Ozawa Forest Road and Uratakao (小沢林道 裏高尾). The ensuing steep climb is one of many along this route, which takes you through forests of cherry trees and past an electricity pylon. Several smaller unmarked trails branch off the narrow path. In places there are good views, and in spring the *tsutsuji* (azalea) growing on the precipitous sides bears pink flowers.

After 40–50 minutes, turn right, in the direction marked "Mt. Hachiōji-shiro via Fujimi Plateau" (富士見台を経て 八王子城山), and then right again at a similarly signposted intersection less than 10 minutes later, after entering a gloomy plantation. In addition to the wildflowers and cherry blossoms in the subsequent area are the ubiquitous red-berried *aoki* (Japanese laurel), which has small, red star-shaped flowers in spring.

Proceed straight through the junction that you meet about 15 minutes later, where the left-hand path leads, via a nearby road, to Kitsune Hill and Hachiōji (狐塚 八王子.) The track then passes close to another forest road before ascending quickly, followed by several quite sudden descents.

Approximately 40 minutes later, turn left in the direction marked "to Hachiōji Castle Site via Castle Lookout Site" (大天主跡 を経て八王子城跡へ), that is, away from the direction "to Kobotoke Checkpoint Site via Fujimi Plateau" (富士見台を経て小仏関所跡へ). This trail has springtime pink *tsubaki* (camellia) flowers and white flowers of the *miyamashikimi* (Japanese star anise) shrub. All that remains of the castle lookout and command post (*daitenshu*, 大天主), which is reached after about 15 minutes, is terraces of roughly cut stone on a rocky outcrop overgrown with trees. A board here tells the grim story of how the besieged defenders of the well-fortified, superbly sited castle waited in vain for reinforcements to arrive before finally committing suicide in desperation.

From Hachiōji Castle Lookout to Zōkei-daigaku-mae (50 minutes)

Continue along the path past the stone monument. There are several more signboards on the way: a stone wall (石垣), architecturally important in the development of castle building; the site of the retainers' residences (家臣屋敷跡); and the "horse cooling" area (馬冷場), where horses rested after arduous rides through the mountainous countryside.

At the junction 10–15 minutes from the castle lookout site, go right, toward the site of Hachiōji Castle (八王子城跡). Turn left, away from Moto-Hachiōji (元八王子) a few minutes later and then right, in both instances in the direction marked "Castle Mountain Summit" (城山山頂). A little higher, just past a small well dating back to the days of the castle, are a large monument and several buildings, including Hachiōji Shrine. To the right of the shrine is a small track that leads the short distance to the summit of Mt. Hachiōji-shiro (*Hachiōji-shiro-yama*). More boards in the area indicate the sites of the castle's main (本丸跡) and secondary (二の丸跡) quarters. Many of the wildflowers at the beginning of this walk are also found here.

To complete this walk, take the wide path signposted "Moto-Hachiōji, direction of Takao Station" (元八王子 高尾駅方面) to the left as you descend the steps from the summit. This is the continuation of the path that runs below the monument and past the viewing area with seats.

In less than 10 minutes, you must choose between the old (至旧道) and new (至新道) paths, the latter of which is described here. Simply follow this path, which eventually becomes much broader, for about 8 minutes downhill to a T-junction with a *torii* (shrine gateway), where you should turn left. Turn right, signposted as "direction for Hachiōji City" (八王子市方面), at the junction with a dirt road after another 100 meters or so. Pass through the nearby second *torii* and walk along the bitumen road, which is straight ahead.

A few hundred meters down this road is Zōkei-daigaku-mae (造形大学前) Bus Terminus on the left. Take the bus from there, getting off at Takao Station (*Takao-eki*, 高尾駅) Bus Stop (5–10 minutes, ¥160). Takao Station is about 100 meters away up the hill. Cross the road at the pedestrian crossing near the bus stop and then go straight ahead.

To return to Shinjuku Station, catch a rapid service train (*kaisoku*, 快速) on the JR Chūō Line (¥530, about 55 minutes), or a limited express or express (*kyūkō*, 急行) on the Keiō Line (¥310, about 50 minutes). The Keiō Line station is on the far side of the JR station.

OKUTAMA

Part of the Chichibu–Tama National Park, the Okutama region offers mountains averaging 1,000 meters in height, deep ravines, limestone caves, and crystal-clear, swift-flowing rivers. Straddling Yamanashi Prefecture and western Tokyo, this delightful area is ideal for appreciating nature in any season. The JR Ōme and Itsukaichi Lines provide convenient access.

Note: A low-cost return (Tokyo Area–Okutama Area–Tokyo) ticket, known as a jiyūkippu, literally "freedom ticket," can be used for destinations anywhere along these lines and is available for ¥1,400 from most JR stations.

13. SENGEN RIDGE ——————————— M

Course: Musashi-Itsukaichi Station (by bus) → Kita-Akikawa-bashi → Hosawa Waterfall → Sengen Peak → Hembori (by bus) → Musashi-Itsukaichi Station

Reference map: Nitchi Map No. 2 (Okutama, 奥多摩), New Series No. 21; or Shōbunsha Map No. 24 (Okutama), New Series No. 24.

Walking time: About 2 hours 50 minutes.

Points of interest: Hosawa Waterfall (particularly in winter), wildflowers (spring to autumn), mountain views, Japanese macaque (winter), an Edo-period track for transporting charcoal.

GETTING THERE

The best way is by direct special rapid service train (*chokutsū tokubetsu kaisoku*, 直通特別快速) from JR Shinjuku Station to Musashi-Itsukaichi (武蔵五日市). Unfortunately, there are only a few of these, which leave from Platform 5 and take 1 hour to 1 hour 10 minutes. Note that only the rear half of the train completes the entire journey to Musashi-Itsukaichi Station, the remaining carriages going to Okutama (奥多摩).

Alternatively, from Platform 8 of the same station, catch a more frequent rapid service train (*kaisoku*, 快速) or special rapid service train (*tokubetsu kaisoku*, 特別快速) to Tachikawa (立川) Station on the Chūō Line (中央線). These take 38 and 27 minutes, respectively. At Tachikawa, change to Platform 2/3, which is the JR Ōme Line (青梅線). It will probably be necessary to change again at Haijima (拝島) Station for the last part of the journey to Musashi-Itsukaichi, the terminus of the Itsukaichi Line (五日市線). From Tachikawa to Musashi-Itsukaichi takes a total of 30–40 minutes, not including connection time.

If you don't purchase a *jiyūkippu* (see page 86), a single ticket from Shinjuku to Musashi-Itsukaichi costs ¥800.

Leave Musashi-Itsukaichi Station by the only exit (retain your *jiyūkippu* if you have one), turn left, walk a few meters to the front of the bus company office, and board a No. 14 bus bound for Kita-Akikawabashi (北秋川橋). The road winds along beside the Aki River and past thatched houses. Get off at the terminus after 20–25 minutes. The fare is ¥410.

From Kita-Akikawabashi to Sengen Peak (2 hours)

Cross the main road and walk along the smaller bitumen-surfaced road that branches off directly opposite. After 20 meters or so, go left down a bitumen lane, just before a bridge. A sign here reads "Hosawa Waterfall" (*Hosawa no taki*, 沸沢の滝). To get to the waterfall, veer left at a fork a few minutes later onto a dirt path also marked for Hosawa Waterfall, though with a simplified first character (払沢の滝). The waterfall is 5–10 minutes along this high rocky path, which crosses several small bridges. In winter, parts of the 60-meter fall and most of the pool at the bottom freeze over, and the icicles hanging off the face make for a splendid sight.

After visiting the waterfall, return to the previous junction, turn hard left in the direction of Sengen Ridge (*Sengen-one*, 浅間尾根). This path merges with a dirt road, which you follow uphill to the large bitumen road and bear left. The trail leaves and rejoins this road several times over the next kilometer or so, and passes many old wooden houses.

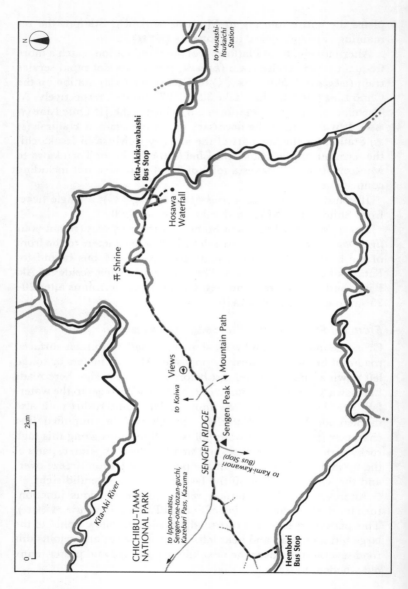

Kita-Akikawabashi
Bus Stop

Hosawa
Waterfall

⛩ Shrine

Views

to Koiwa

Mountain Path

SENGEN RIDGE

▲ Sengen Peak

to Kami-kawanori
(bus stop)

to Ippon-matsu,
Sengen-one-tozan-guchi;
Kazebari Pass, Kazuma

Kita-Aki River

CHICHIBU–TAMA
NATIONAL PARK

Hembori
Bus Stop

to Musashi-
Itsukaichi Station

N

0   1   2km

Thatched farmhouse near Sengen Ridge.

A few minutes further on, at the sign for "Jizaka Pass, Sengen Peak" (時坂峠 浅間嶺), take the steps up to the left. Rejoin the road 10 minutes later, again heading uphill to the left. The path (similarly signposted) resumes sharply to the left after about 10 more minutes. From here it zigzags up the hill, crossing the road (at a similar sign) after 5 minutes. The path soon bends left (near a tiny shrine), and begins to trace the line of Sengen Ridge, merging with the dirt road that enters from the left after 5–10 minutes. A sign here indicates that straight ahead is Sengen Peak and Kami-Kawanori Bus Stop (上川乗バス停). Follow this road for about 10 minutes until it ends at a building. The path continues to the left.

Walking for 7 minutes or so will bring you to a magnificent and rather photogenic old farmhouse with a thatched roof, rustic sheds, and a water supply system consisting of lengths of bamboo split in half to form open pipes, which are joined together and connected to a nearby stream.

Ascend steeply for 30–40 minutes, first next to a small stream and past rock pools, and later through a forest with broad-leaved magnolia trees (and where orange fungi used in a herbal cancer treatment can be found). There are also many wildflowers at various times of the year, such as summer *yamayuri* (gold-banded lily).

After passing a more open area with fine views of such nearby peaks as Mt. Gozen, you come to a junction marked "Mountain Path" (山道) to the left and Koiwa (小岩), from where a bus leaves for Musashi-Itsukaichi, to the right. Continue straight ahead. Less than 10 minutes later, you arrive at an junction next to a small camping and picnic area that is suitable for lunch, with tables and chairs, a shelter, a fireplace, and toilets.

A small path next to a map board here leads to Sengen Peak, also known as Mt. Hinobara, the highest point (904 meters above sea level) on Sengen Ridge. The map board provides some history of the area, as follows:

KANTŌ COMMUNITY ROADS
Historical Path

The 8-kilometer route from Kami-Kawanori to Hon-juku leads up in the direction of Sengen Ridge and traverses Jizaka Pass. Passing through the middle of the Hinobara-mura area and tracing the comparatively moderate lie of the land, Sengen-one Road, also called Naka-Kōshū Road, has from olden times been an important traffic thoroughfare. During the Edo period, it was an important route for hauling charcoal by horse and for the transport of daily necessities. Besides the village folk, people from Ogochi and Nishihara also used the trail.

Another interesting feature of the area is the presence of Japanese macaque, which descend in winter from the cold upper reaches of the surrounding mountains to these slopes. They are quite shy and are more likely to be sighted on the southern side of the ridge.

From Sengen Peak to Hembori (50 minutes)

Return to the signposted junction near the shelter and take the main trail in the direction you were walking, that is, toward Kazebari Pass and Hembori Bus Stop (風張峠 人里バス停). The other track leads to Kami-Kawanori Bus Stop, as indicated on the sign. At a T-junction 10–15 minutes later, there is a choice of routes.

To extend this walk, proceed straight through this junction in the direction of Kazebari Pass and Kazuma (風張峠 数馬) via Ippon-matsu (一本松, literally, "One Pine Tree"), and then turn south down to Sengen-one-tozan-guchi (浅間尾根登山口) Bus Stop. The bus

Mountain village in Okutama panorama.

trip from there to Musashi-Itsukaichi Station costs ¥830 and lasts less than 55 minutes.

If you don't want to extend the walk, turn left toward Hembori (人里) at the T-junction. After 5 more minutes you go straight through another T-junction, this time toward Hembori-Kotonuki (人里 事貫). (Don't turn left, as this leads to another part of the Hembori area, signposted as 人里 和田.) From here, simply follow the Hembori Bus Stop (人里バス停) signs for about 25 minutes, keeping to the left through several junctions and passing a mountain lodge with an adjacent bamboo stand, to a concrete road near some tea plantations. You take this road down past a few houses to the main road. Hembori Bus Stop is immediately to your right.

The bus ride to Musashi-Itsukaichi Station takes about 45 minutes, and the fare is ¥750. To return to Shinjuku Station, it is best to take the direct special rapid service train, but in any case follow in reverse the instructions provided in the "Getting There" section for this walk (use your *jiyūkippu*, if you have one).

14. THE THREE PEAKS OF TAKAMIZU – M

Course: Mitake Station → Mt. Sōgaku → Mt. Iwatakeishi → Mt. Takamizu → Ikusabata Station

Reference map: Nitchi Map No. 2 (Okutama, 奥多摩), New Series No. 21; or Shōbunsha Map No. 24 (Okutama), New Series No. 24.

Walking time: About 3 hours 20 minutes.

Points of interest: Aoi Shrine and Jōfuku Temple, and good views of the three rugged peaks of Takamizu.

GETTING THERE

The best way is to take a direct special rapid service train (*chokutsū tokubetsu kaisoku*, 直通特別快速) from JR Shinjuku Station bound for Okutama (奥多摩) Station. Alight at Mitake (御嶽) Station. Unfortunately, there are only a few of these trains, which leave from Platform 5 and take about 1 hour 15 minutes. Note that only the front half of the train goes to Okutama, the other carriages going to Musashi-Itsukaichi (武蔵五日市).

Alternatively, from Platform 8 of the same station, take a more frequent rapid service train (*kaisoku*, 快速) or special rapid service train (*tokubetsu kaisoku*, 特別快速) to Tachikawa (立川) Station on the Chūō Line (中央線) (38 and 27 minutes, respectively). At Tachikawa, change to Platform 2/3, which is the JR Ōme Line (青梅線) for the train to Mitake Station (about 50 minutes). If you don't have an Okutama *jiyūkippu* (see page 86), the single fare from Shinjuku to Mitake is ¥930.

From Mitake Station to Mt. Sōgaku (1 hour 20 minutes)

Leave Mitake Station by the only exit (retain your *jiyūkippu* if you have one), turn left at the main road, and walk for about 30 meters to stairs painted yellow on the step edges. Climb these, and cross the railway line at the top. A sign at the side of the small road here indicates the way to Mt. Sōgaku and Mt. Iwatakeishi (惣岳山 岩茸石山). Cross the road, walk up the path leading to the entrance of the building immediately opposite, and then follow the small concrete path that runs to the left of the building.

The ascent of Mt. Sōgaku (Sōgaku-san) consists of a series of short climbs, with an occasional downward stretch. Stay on the main path and avoid any smaller tracks. Initially, the path winds up a steep rocky slope through dark *hinoki* (cypress) forest, but it soon flattens out, passing several electricity pylons and concrete benches as it follows a ridge that is a spur of Mt. Sōgaku. In places the forest has been felled, allowing views of the cone-shaped Mt. Honida to the left.

Some 30–35 minutes after leaving Mitake Station, following a section that descends you reach a junction with tracks to Tannawa (丹縄) to the left, and to Sawai Station (沢井駅) to the right. Continue straight ahead.

The path begins to rise again, past another pylon, more benches, and a large clearing, before entering native forest that includes magnificently tall trees. After a further 40 minutes or so, a signposted trail leads to the right at a T-junction—this trail skirts the summit of Mt. Sōgaku. However, keep to the left, toward Mt. Sōgaku and Mt. Iwatakeishi, and in less than 10 minutes you arrive at Aoi Shrine at the top.

Legend has it that during the Heian period (794–1192) a general on his way to fight the Taira clan was passing the nearby Tama River when the waters turned blue (*aoi*), which was interpreted as a good omen, hence the name of the shrine. The shrine was originally constructed in the tenth century, and even the current structure is over a hundred years old and has fine carvings adorning the wooden eaves. Unfortunately, the building is now fenced off to protect it.

The summit of Mt. Sōgaku is surrounded by tall trees that obstruct the views, so it is better to walk on to Mt. Iwatakeishi before stopping for lunch.

From Mt. Sōgaku to Ikusabata Station (2 hours)

Walk down the other side of Mt. Sōgaku by taking the path to the right of the shrine, signposted for Mt. Iwatakeishi and Mt. Kuro (岩茸石山 山黒山). The descent is extremely steep, so you should walk carefully. The trees in this area are old and very beautiful, and some have superbly contorted roots that are exposed on the rocky

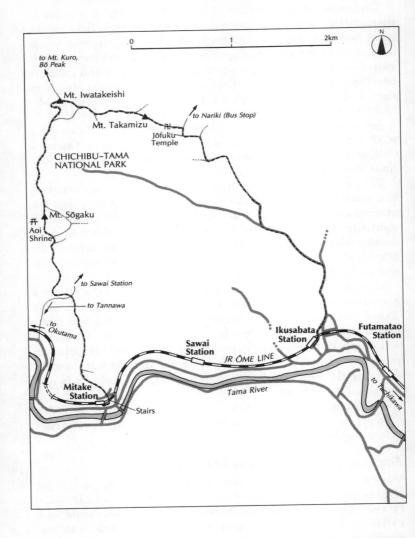

slope. At the bottom of the slope, go straight ahead, ignoring the path that joins from the right, which is the other end of the path that skirts the summit of Mt. Sōgaku.

This trail is one of the "Community Roads in the Kantō Area" (*Kantō fureai no michi*) that have been marked for hikers, and it follows a ridge through cedar forest to the edge of Mt. Iwatakeishi. Ahead and to the right are magnificent views of rugged Mt. Iwatakeishi and Mt. Takamizu, which with Mt. Sōgaku make up the three peaks of Takamizu (*Takamizu sanzan*). Keep on the main path, following signs for Mt. Iwatakeishi and Mt. Kuro, for about 30 minutes, until you come to a junction near a rocky outcrop. You can go either way, but I suggest you veer left, away from Mt. Takamizu and Ikusabata Station (高水山 軍畑駅), to ascend Mt. Iwatakeishi (*Iwatakeishiyama*). A 10-minute climb will bring you to the summit, with views of both the nearby mountains and the densely populated Kantō Plain. At 793 meters, this is the highest of the three peaks, and it is a good place for lunch.

To leave the summit, ignore the sign pointing left to Mt. Kuro (*Kuroyama*, 黒山) and Bō Peak (*Bō-no-mine*, 棒の嶺)—a walk to which is described in the Okumusashi section—and go slightly to the right down the other side toward Mt. Takamizu and Ikusabata Station. The detour around the summit of Mt. Iwatakeishi joins from the right within 10 minutes. At a fork with a nearby concrete bench shortly after, keep to the left, again toward Mt. Takamizu and Ikusabata Station. Due to its northerly aspect, in winter the path here is frequently eroded by subsoil water freezing into large ice crystals, which make an unusual sight when they literally break open the surface.

After 10 minutes, at another fork, go straight uphill in the direction marked "Mt. Takamizu Summit, Ikusabata Station" (高水山 山頂 軍畑駅). Close by, at the top of this rocky slope that has tree roots covered in fungus, is the summit of Mt. Takamizu (*Takamizu-san*), with a sweeping view across in the direction of Mt. Gozen.

Continue slightly to the left down the other side in the direction marked "Ikusabata Station, Nariki Bus Stop" (軍畑駅 成木バス停), and in a few minutes you will be in the compound of the beautiful

Wooden swords guard the entrance to Jōfuku Temple.

Jōfuku Temple. Across the entrance to the main hall are large wooden swords, placed as a protection against evil. The temple is dedicated to Fudō, one of the Buddhist kings of light and wisdom who is also associated with fire.

Leave by the main gate, go down the stone steps and turn right in the direction of Ikusabata Station (軍畑駅). Bear left shortly after and then right a few minutes later at similarly signposted T-junctions.

From here, simply note the direction of the signs for the station as you descend this steep rocky slope covered in cedar forest. Just after passing fish-cultivation tanks some 20–25 minutes from the previous junction, you reach a concrete road. Take this road downhill, past fields and tea plantations. Near a temple the road merges with another from the right and yet another from the left, 15–20 minutes after the tanks. Keep going downhill along the bitumen road next to the stream. After a few minutes, you will see a small road (signposted for the station) leading uphill to the right, and an iron railway bridge should be visible ahead. Follow this small road for a few minutes across the railway line and then to the right, to the station.

The train to Tachikawa along this single-track line takes about 45 minutes. If the station is unmanned and you don't have a *jiyūkippu*, obtain a green slip by pressing the button on the machine on the platform and pay for your ticket on the train or at your destination (from Ikusabata to Shinjuku costs ¥930). Make sure you get on a train going to your right as you face the railway line, which is the direction of Tachikawa. At Tachikawa, change to the Chūō Line for Shinjuku.

15. MT. MITAKE ——————— D

Course: Kori Station → Mt. Ōtsuka → Mt. Mitake → Mt. Hinode⌐ Hinatawada Station
⌐ Yōsawa Stalactite Cave → Kami-Yōsawa
Bus Stop (by bus) → Musashi-Itsukaichi Station

Reference map: Nitchi Map No. 2 (Okutama, 奥多摩), New Series No. 21; or Shōbunsha Map No. 24 (Okutama), New Series No. 24.

Walking time: About 4 hours 45 minutes (excluding alternative route).

Points of interest: Leafy forests and mountain views, Mitake Shrine, and, on an alternative path, Yōsawa Stalactite Cave.

GETTING THERE

From Platform 8 of JR Shinjuku Station, catch a rapid service train (*kaisoku*, 快速) or special rapid service train (*tokubetsu kaisoku*, 特別快速) on the JR Chūō Line (中央線) to Tachikawa (立川) Station (38 and 27 minutes, respectively). At Tachikawa, change to Platform 2/3, which is the JR Ōme Line (青梅線) to Okutama, and take a train to Kori (古里) Station.

Not all trains stop at or go as far as Kori, so make sure by asking or checking the timetable that you are getting on the right one. From Tachikawa to Kori takes about 1 hour by local service. For those without an Okutama *jiyūkippu* (see page 86), a one-way Shinjuku–Kori ticket costs ¥930.

From Kori Station to Mt. Ōtsuka (1 hour 30 minutes)

After passing through the ticket barrier at Kori Station (retain your *jiyūkippu* if you have one), walk straight ahead to the main road. In front of you are a pedestrian crossing and a corner "convenience" store. Cross the road and follow the other road that runs to the left of the store, traversing a bridge high over the scenic Tama River. This road passes some old houses with thatched roofs.

After approximately 10 minutes, you will notice a small con-

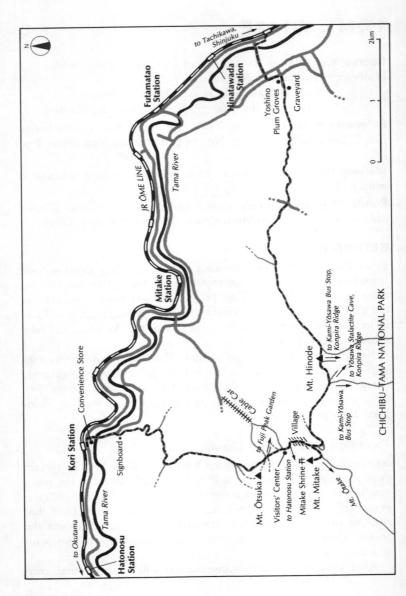

crete road veering uphill to the right. A sign here says "Mt. Ōtsuka and Mt. Mitake mountain climbing access" (大塚山 御岳山 登山口). After a few paces, the concrete road turns directly uphill and soon becomes a walking track.

The first half of this ascent is quite steep, but on a clear day you will be rewarded with good views of the Okutama mountains and native forests. In autumn, these forests are truly a blaze of reds and oranges before the leaves begin to fall.

Follow any signs for Mt. Ōtsuka, the immediate destination, and Mt. Mitake. Within 20 minutes, you come to an unmarked fork. Take the right-hand uphill path. Some 30 minutes later, at another fork, veer left. The other path is labelled a "mountain track" (山道).

After another 30 minutes, a choice of three paths will present itself. The center one leads the short distance to the 921-meter-high summit of Mt. Ōtsuka (*Ōtsukayama*), where there are the graves of some Buddhist priests, but to continue take the left-hand path.

From Mt. Ōtsuka to Mt. Hinode via Mt. Mitake (1 hour 5 minutes)

A little further on is another junction, this time with five alternatives. Immediately to the left (ケーブル駅) is the route to the upper terminus of the Mt. Mitake cable car, while the central uphill track climbs to Fuji Peak Garden (富士峰園地). Take the path slightly to the right, marked "Mitake Shrine, Nagao Plain Garden" (御嶽神社 長尾平園地) and "Course Eight" (エイトコース).

Some 5–10 minutes later, after passing a larger track that joins from the left, this path descends to merge with a paved lane that leads into the village near the summit of Mt. Mitake (*Mitake-san*). Immediately on your right is a visitors' center with a good display on the local topography, flora, and fauna. There will most likely be a noticeable increase in the number of fellow walkers from this point on, at least until Mt. Hinode, since many people take the cable car up.

To reach Mitake Shrine (*Mitake-jinja*, 御嶽神社), follow the Course Eight and Mt. Hinode (日ノ出山) signs for about 10 minutes along the paved lane that winds down and then up between houses, shops, and souvenir stalls. You should pass the beginning

Mitake Shrine.

of a path on the right to Hatonosu Station (鳩ノ巣駅). As the shrine
is located on the summit of Mt. Mitake, take the uphill (right-
hand) Course Eight path where the lane splits, that is, away from
Mt. Hinode. Near the shrine entrance, the Course Eight path
branches to the left toward Mt. Ōtake (大岳山), but continue up the
steps.

Mitake Shrine has something of an interesting history. Found-
ed two hundred years ago under the protection of the Tokugawa
shogunate, it was reconstructed during the Meiji period (1868–
1912). In one part of the complex are national treasures that include swords, armor, mirrors, and documents. Entry to this
building costs ¥200. On May 8 each year, the shrine festival
(*Hinode matsuri*) is held, consisting of a parade of portable shrines
and samurai warriors in full armor. Mitake Shrine or one of the
nearby restaurants that serve *sansaisoba* (mountain vegetable
noodles) and *tororosoba* (noodles with grated mountain yam) is a
pleasant place for lunch with a view, or else you can walk on to
Mt. Hinode.

Note that, since it takes a relatively short time (7 minutes,
¥450) to descend by cable car from the upper terminus and to then
reach Mitake (御嶽) Station on the Ōme Line by bus (7 minutes,
¥230), Kori Station → Mitake Shrine → Mitake Station is a
shortened walk for those who don't wish to complete the entire
course. To reach the cable car station, follow the signs back along
the concrete path past the visitors' center.

After leaving the shrine, return to the junction with the sign for Mt. Hinode and turn hard right in that direction. Take the lower of the two paths and then turn left onto the main path for Mt. Hinode, keeping to the right soon after and following the signs. Among the late spring and early summer flowers common on trails in this area are white-and-pink *yukinoshita* (strawberry geranium or mother-of-thousands), blue *ajisai* (hydrangea), white and purple *koajisai* (a type of hydrangea with clusters of small flowers), yellow *sawagiku* (marsh chrysanthemum), white *chidakesashi* (*Astilbe microphylla*), and white and yellow *suikazura* (Japanese honeysuckle).

A little short of the summit of Mt. Hinode are two junctions within a few meters of each other—keep to the left, that is, uphill, on both occasions. The first path passed leads to Kami-Yōsawa Bus Stop (上養沢駅バス停), and the second to Yōsawa Stalactite Cave and Konpira Ridge via a short cut (養沢鐘乳洞 金比羅尾根近道). From Mitake Shrine to the open top of Mt. Hinode (*Hinodeyama*) will take about 40 minutes. The summit rises 902 meters above sea level (almost the same as Mt. Ōtsuka and Mt. Mitake) and offers breathtaking 360° views, although sometimes it gets crowded.

From here the main walk described is to Hinatawada (日向和田) Station on the Ōme Line, but it is also possible to visit Yōsawa and other limestone caves, and then make your way to Kami-Yōsawa Bus Stop and so to Musashi-Itsukaichi Station. For this alternative route, see the last section of this walk.

From Mt. Hinode to Hinatawada Station (2 hours 10 minutes)

Walk straight down the other side of the summit, in the direction signposted for "Mt. Mitsumuro, Futamatao Station" (三室山 二俣尾駅). Follow the main path, which is downhill and quite easy going, and any signs for Hinatawada Station, past several turnoffs. About 50 minutes after leaving the top of Mt. Hinode, the trail becomes a road, with a small fenced installation to the left. Shortly, another road will cut across your path. Keep going straight ahead onto the unpaved path. Just before meeting the road leading into the town of Hinatawada, the path skirts a golf course carved into the hillside.

The walk down the road to Hinatawada is noteworthy for the

old houses, bonsai nursery, park, and graveyard on the right, and the Yoshino plum groves (吉野梅郷) in an area to the left, some 20,000 trees of which bloom in the middle of March.

On reaching the main road, turn left, and then right at the traffic lights about 100 meters further on. Follow this road across the bridge and turn right. Hinatawada Station is on the left. Return home via Tachikawa. A one-way Hinatawada–Shinjuku ticket costs ¥800. (If you bought an Okutama *jiyūkippu*, use this for the return journey.)

From Mt. Hinode to Kami-Yōsawa
via Yōsawa Stalactite Cave (1 hour 15 minutes)

To reach Yōsawa Stalactite Cave (養沢鐘乳洞), take the path from the summit, marked "Kami-Yōsawa Bus Stop, Konpira Ridge" (上養沢バス停金比羅尾根), to the right. Follow similar signs for 40–50 minutes downhill. The cave is visible from the trail, past a small caretaker's building. Admission costs ¥300, and for this you get the use of a torch and candle. Although the total length of the cave is only about 50 meters, clambering up and down the series of wooden ladders to explore the multichambered cavern makes it seem a good deal larger. There are several other limestone caves (Ōtake, 大岳 and Mitsugo, 三子) in the general area. To complete this alternative walk, it is best to continue downhill from the cave for about 10 minutes to the bitumen road, where you should bear left. About 20 minutes further is Kami-Yōsawa Bus Stop, the terminus of the bus to Musashi-Itsukaichi (武蔵五日市) Station on the JR Itsukaichi Line (五日市線). The 30-minute bus ride costs ¥410 and the one-way train fare to Shinjuku (via Haijima and Tachikawa) is ¥800, though you can use your Okutama *jiyūkippu* for the return journey if you have one.

Yōsawa Stalactite Cave.

16. MT. GOZEN ——————————————— D

Course: Okutama Station (by bus) → Sakaibashi → Mt. Gozen → Miyagayato (by bus) → Musashi-Itsukaichi Station

Reference map: Nitchi Map No. 2 (Okutama, 奥多摩), New Series No. 21; or Shōbunsha Map No. 24 (Okutama), New Series No. 24.

Walking time: About 5 hours.

Points of interest: Tochiyori Valley, with its deciduous forests, mountain views, autumn colors, and spring wildflowers.

GETTING THERE

The best way is to go by a direct special rapid service train (*chokutsū tokubetsu kaisoku*, 直通特別快速) from JR Shinjuku Station to Okutama (奥多摩) Station. Unfortunately, there only a few of these trains, which leave from Platform 5 and take about 1 hour 30 minutes. Note that only the front half of the train completes the entire journey to Okutama, the remaining carriages going to Musashi-Itsukaichi (武蔵五日市).

Alternatively, from Platform 8 of the same station, catch a more frequent rapid service train (*kaisoku*, 快速) or special rapid service train (*tokubetsu kaisoku*, 特別快速) on the Chūō Line (中央線) to Tachikawa (立川) Station (38 and 27 minutes, respectively). At Tachikawa, change to Platform 2/3, which is the JR Ōme Line (青梅線), and ride to the terminus at Okutama (about 1 hour 10 minutes). If you don't have an Okutama *jiyūkippu* (see page 86), the single fare from Shinjuku to Okutama is ¥1,090.

Leave Okutama Station by the only exit (retain your *jiyūkippu* if you have one), walk across the road to Bus Stand No. 2, and board any bus. The scenic route takes you over arch bridges spanning yawning chasms and the upper reaches of the Tama River. In autumn there are splendid views of mountain slopes swathed with mantles of red and yellow leaves. After about 10 minutes, get off at Sakaibashi (境橋) Bus Stop, which is on a bridge. The fare is ¥190.

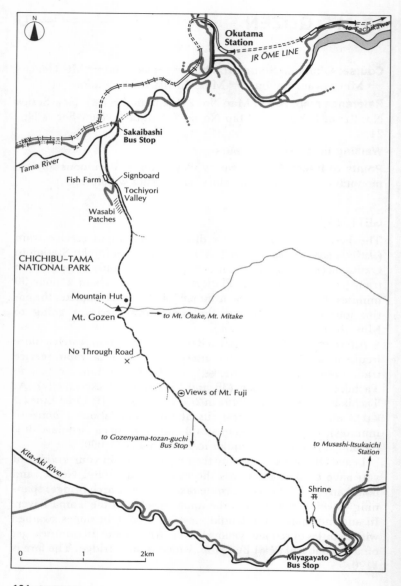

N

to Tachikawa

Okutama Station

JR ŌME LINE

Sakaibashi Bus Stop

Tama River

Fish Farm Signboard

Tochiyori Valley

Wasabi Patches

CHICHIBU–TAMA NATIONAL PARK

Mountain Hut

Mt. Gozen → *to Mt. Ōtake, Mt. Mitake*

No Through Road ×

⊖ Views of Mt. Fuji

to Gozenyama-tozan-guchi Bus Stop

to Musashi-Itsukaichi Station

Shrine 卍

Kita-Aki River

0   1   2km

Miyagayato Bus Stop

From Sakaibashi to Mt. Gozen (2 hours 30 minutes)

Walk back on the same side of the road in the direction from which you have come. Take the gravel road that branches off to the right after 100 meters or so, just before a tunnel. This road is quite steep, as is most of the climb up Mt. Gozen (*Gozenyama*, 御前 山), and it follows the Tochiyori Valley. There are many wildflowers on these slopes, particularly in spring, including various kinds of *azami* (thistle) and daisy. Small yellow *kosen-dangusa* (Spanish needles) and *yakushisō* (hawk's beard) are common in late summer and autumn.

Some 20 minutes from the start of the road, just after a fish farm, a small path leads off to the left at a curve in the road. It is clearly indicated by a signboard reading "Mt. Gozen mountain climbing access" (御前山登山口). This steep and rocky path, which you should follow, has few major junctions before the summit, and ascends via a narrow valley with deciduous forests, through which a small stream flows. In autumn, this valley becomes a series of picturesque leafy hollows. There are many rotting makeshift bridges along the way, and care should be taken on these, with one person crossing at a time. Another feature of the valley is the many raked-gravel *wasabi* (Japanese horseradish) patches, some terraced, along the early stages of the track.

About 30 minutes from the start of the path, you pass a particularly attractive grotto where a stream pours down into a pool between two large rocks—a good place for a photo and a rest.

Ignore any minor tracks veering off to the left. The final part of the ascent involves a hike directly up the northern slope of Mt. Gozen that is fairly arduous but, with the many pine trees and ferns, is also very scenic.

In about 1 hour you reach a small mountain hut with a well next to it. A few minutes past the hut is a signposted junction. The path to the left goes to the well-known Mt. Ōtake and Mt. Mitake (a walk to which is described in the Okutama section). Instead, turn to the right (至御前山 月夜見山 三頭山 on the signpost), which leads to the 1,405-meter summit of Mt. Gozen, some 10–15 minutes away. Due to the tree cover, it is possible to get good views of the surrounding ranges only in autumn and winter when the trees are bare.

Wasabi patch in the Tochiyori Valley.

Mt. Gozen is famous for the beautiful *katakuri* (dogtooth violet) that grows underground for nine months and blooms in April. Other spring flowers in the area include *fuderindō* (gentian), *nirinsō* (anemone), *charumerusō* (miterwort), and *rempukusō* (moschatel).

From Mt. Gozen to Miyagayato (2 hours 30 minutes)

Return to the junction near the summit and take the path to the right, indicated on the signpost as 至湯久保尾根 桧原村小沢. As the last part of the second group of characters is the name of your general destination, Ozawa (小沢), simply heed the similarly labelled signs at the various junctions and just stay on the main path. The path to Ozawa is mostly downhill, cutting initially through deciduous forest and later through *sugi* (cedar) plantations. This trail at times follows the ridges, and here also is a wealth of wildflowers. Blue *rindō* (another kind of gentian) is particularly abundant in autumn.

About 25 minutes from the summit junction is a tiny shelter and a path to the right, marked "No Through Road" (この先行止り). Pass by this and continue downhill in the direction of Ozawa. You come to two junctions, the first, which is signposted, after about 15 minutes and the second a few minutes later. Continue straight through both of these, toward Ozawa. The path climbs briefly from here, through more pine trees. From the top of the ridge, you have uninterrupted views of Mt. Fuji.

At a junction about 20 minutes further on, shortly after entering a cedar plantation, a path marked "to Gozenyama-tozan-guchi Bus Stop (about 70 minutes)" (至御前山登山口バス停約70分) leads off to the right. Ignore it and continue straight ahead, down the ridge.

Pass straight through another unmarked junction after 10 minutes, and then, after a further 10 minutes, another with the sign "short cut to Ozawa Bus Stop" (小沢バス停近道) attached to a tree. In fact, it is possible to go either way. The steep, rocky track to the right takes you past a pile of logs where *shiitake* (mushrooms) are cultivated, a small shelter, a small path to the right, and some buildings and cultivated areas. In 10 minutes, the paths rejoin. Continue straight, indicated "to Miyagayato Bus Stop" (至宮ヶ谷戸バス停). The trail again traces the line of the ridges. Avoid any small paths leading off.

Some 30–40 minutes later, at some stone tablets, the path intersects with another leading to a shrine. The path to the left leads to the shrine—a *torii* (Shinto shrine gateway) can be seen down the right-hand path. Go straight, and in 10 minutes the trail emerges at a road. Miyagayato (宮ヶ谷戸) Bus Stop is only a few minutes from here. Follow this road downhill past houses and fields, along whose edges *inutade* (red-beaded knotgrass) grows in autumn, turn right, then left, and cross the Kita-Aki River to the main road. The bus stop is a few meters to the left.

The bus trip to Musashi-Itsukaichi (武蔵五日市) Station on the JR Itsukaichi Line (五日市線) costs ¥530 and takes about 40 minutes. To return to Shinjuku Station, it is best to take a direct train. Otherwise, take a train to Tachikawa, changing if necessary at Haijima (拝島) on the Ōme Line. At Tachikawa, change to the Chūō Line for Shinjuku. The fare for the entire journey is ¥800. (If you purchased an Okutama *jiyūkippu*, use this for the return trip.)

OKUMUSASHI

The Okumusashi region of Saitama Prefecture to the northwest of Tokyo consists mainly of relatively low mountains and hills, many of which are covered with cedar and cypress plantations. It will therefore suit those who prefer to walk in country that is not so mountainous. Areas of special interest include the Okumusashi and Kuroyama Prefectural Natural Parks. Most trails are readily accessible from Tokyo, in particular from Ikebukuro Station by means of the Seibu Ikebukuro and Tōbu Tōjō lines.

17. KAMI-DAIMA TO OGOSE ———— E

Course: Ogose Station (by bus) → Kami-Daima → Mt. Katsuragi → Mt. Ōtakatori → Mt. Takatori → Ogose Station

Reference map: Nitchi Map No. 1 (Okumusashi, 奥武蔵), New Series No. 20; or Shōbunsha Map No. 25 (Okumusashi Chichibu, 奥武蔵 秩父), New Series No. 25.

Walking time: About 2 hours.

Points of interest: Katsuragi Kannon Temple, spring and summer wildflowers.

GETTING THERE

At Ikebukuro Station, board a Tōbu Tōjō Line (東武東上線) limited express (*tokkyū*, 特急) or express (*kyūkō*, 急行) bound for Shinrin-kōen (森林公園) or Ogawamachi (小川町), and get off at Sakado (坂戸) Station. These trains take 41 and 45 minutes, respectively.

At Sakado, change to the Ogose branch line (越生線), which starts from Platform 2/3. Take any train to the terminus, Ogose (越生) Station, a journey lasting 18 minutes. The total fare is ¥600.

It is also possible to reach Ogose by the JR Hachikō Line (八高線) via Hachiōji (八王子) and Hajima (拝島).

In front of Ogose Station, catch a Tōbu (東武) bus for Kuroyama

(黒山), and after about 15 minutes get off at Kami-Daima (上大満). The fare is ¥230.

From Kami-Daima to Mt. Ōtakatori (55 minutes)

Walk down the small lane leading off to the left at the bus stop, just before a bridge. In less than 100 meters, on the right between a building and a pole with a small NHK sign, you should see a narrow path leading to a pedestrian bridge without handrails that spans the small river. Cross the river and turn left along the road on the other side.

Within a minute or two, veer right up the gravel vehicle track that leaves the road at a bend. This road runs adjacent to a minor stream and is excellent for viewing late spring and early summer wildflowers, including several kinds of daisy, white *shirotsumekusa* (Dutch clover) and *dokudami* (*Houttuynia cordata*), thistles, dandelions, and pink *kohirugao* (convolvulus). Also common in this area are *gishigishi* (sorrel), white-flowered deutzia trees, white and yellow *suikazura* (Japanese honeysuckle), and various wild strawberries and raspberries, among them the yellow-flowered *hebiichigo* (Indian strawberry) and tasty *kusaichigo*.

After 10–15 minutes, the gravel track ends at a clearing where two small paths branch off. Follow the right-hand path, which also follows the route of a small stream, into planted forest. Beside the path are ferns and *aoki* (laurel) trees. Stay on the main path, which soon traverses the stream and then heads directly uphill. A little later, the path splits into two. Both paths have the same destination, but the left-hand one is a little easier to negotiate.

At the top of the slope, another track joins from the right, but continue straight on. Wildflowers, such as yellow *hahakogusa* (cotton- or cudweed) and mauve *niwazekishō* (blue-eyed grass), are also common along this section of the trail, which passes several clearings and an orchard. This region is known for its *yuzu* (citron or Chinese lemon), plums, and sweet *fukumikan* (a kind of mandarin orange).

About 20 minutes from the end of the gravel vehicle track, a wide path veers uphill to the left. Although you can go in either direction, follow this upper route between houses and cultivated plots to the beginning of a bitumen road a few minutes away.

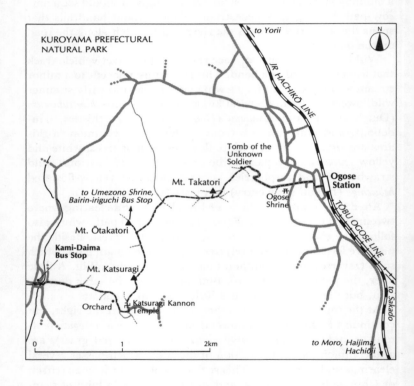

KUROYAMA PREFECTURAL NATURAL PARK

to Yorii

JR HACHIKŌ LINE

Tomb of the Unknown Soldier

Mt. Takatori

to Umezono Shrine, Bairin-iriguchi Bus Stop

Ogose Shrine

Ogose Station

Mt. Ōtakatori

TŌBU OGOSE LINE

Kami-Daima Bus Stop

Mt. Katsuragi

Orchard

Katsuragi Kannon Temple

to Sakado

0   1   2km

to Moro, Haijima, Hachiōji

Proceed along the road, and after 100 meters turn left up the stone steps signposted "Ogose Station via Mt. Ōtakatori" (大高取山を経て越生駅). The steps lead to Katsuragi Kannon Temple, dedicated to Senju Kannon, the Thousand-handed Goddess of Mercy. Near the top of the steps is an old bell under a thatched roof, and through the gate is the temple itself. This building, reputed to have been originally built in Heian times (794–1192), has colorful painted carvings of mythical beasts on its eaves. Views of the area from this point are good, which makes it a suitable place for taking a break or having lunch.

The wide path to Mt. Katsuragi continues from the right side of the rear of the temple grounds, past some toilets. The trail skirts a few buildings on its way through cedar plantations where white and purple *koajisai* (a kind of hydrangea with clusters of small flowers) flourishes. The summit of Mt. Katsuragi (桂木山) is just 10 minutes from Katsuragi Kannon Temple and is identified by a sign on a tree.

From Mt. Katsuragi to Ogose Station (1 hour 5 minutes)

The view from Mt. Katsuragi is limited, so walk down the other side, which has mixed forest, particularly on the left. About 5 minutes along is a board identifying by their silhouettes the peaks and other landmarks visible on a clear day. Nearby is a sign indicating that this is the path to the Tomb of the Unknown Soldier and to Ogose Station (無名戦士の墓 越生駅).

The trail then enters a dense, dark plantation before climbing to the 376-meter-high summit of Mt. Ōtakatori (*Ōtakatoriyama*, 大高取山), approximately 10 minutes away. The continuation of the trail to Mt. Takatori, which is lower than Mt. Ōtakatori, branches off to the right through an area relatively cleared of undergrowth about 100 meters before the top. The summit is worth visiting for the westerly views.

Although I will not describe it in detail here, the right-hand one of the two somewhat overgrown paths down the other side of this peak leads to Umezono Shrine and Bairin-iriguchi Bus Stop, which you passed in the bus on the way to Kami-Daima. Both these tracks have many berried plants, including edible *miyamanigaichigo* and sweet, amber *momijiichigo* raspberries in summer.

Carvings at Katsuragi
Kannon Temple.

When you leave the summit, return to the junction just below it and turn left along the wide but unsignposted downward path. From here the trail wanders up and down across a series of low hills and passes the remains of a small quarry on the left. Stay on the main path, following signs for the Tomb of the Unknown Soldier and Ogose Station.

After 20–25 minutes, you reach a four-way junction, signposted for the Tomb of the Unknown Soldier and Ogose Station, with steps leading up to the left. Climb these steps to the edge of the summit of Mt. Takatori (*Takatoriyama*, 高取山), where there are rough log benches for resting or having lunch on. To the right are good views of the town of Moro.

To reach the Tomb of the Unknown Soldier, continue through the junction near the benches and down the steep signposted path, slightly to the left, on the other side. After just 10 minutes, the trail enters the tomb grounds from the rear. This memorial, whose full name is "Tomb of the Universal Unknown Soldier" (世界無名戦士の墓), is a white semicircular building with a balcony that offers good views of the old town of Ogose. On the ground floor is a small shrine.

Go down the steps at the front of the building in the direction signposted for Ogose Shrine (正法 越生神社), and then walk down the concrete road immediately in front. This winds past a Zen temple, an alternative path from Mt. Takatori, and, finally, Ogose Shrine. Continue straight ahead along the bitumen road through the streets of Ogose to where, some 15 minutes from the tomb, you meet the main road at a T-junction. Turn right, and then left at the traffic lights after 50 meters. Ogose Station is 50 meters farther on.

To return to Ikebukuro, follow in reverse the instructions in the "Getting There" section for this walk.

18. MT. TENKAKU AND MT. ŌTAKA — M

Course: Higashi-Agano Station → Mt. Tenkaku → Mt. Ōtaka → Maesaka → Agano Station

Reference map: Nitchi Map No. 1 (Okumusashi, 奥武蔵), New Series No. 20; or Shōbunsha Map No. 25 (Okumusashi Chichibu, 奥武蔵 秩父), New Series No. 25.

Walking time: About 3 hours 15 minutes.

Points of interest: Views of the Naguri area and the Okutama mountains, and spring wildflowers.

GETTING THERE

From Ikebukuro Station, it is best to take a rapid express (*kaisoku kyūkō*, 快速特急) bound for Seibu-Chichibu (西武秩父) on the Seibu Ikebukuro Line (西武池袋線). Get off at Higashi-Agano (東吾野), a quiet little town nestling in the Koma River valley. The journey takes about 1 hour 5 minutes. In the absence of a direct train, catch an express (*kyūkō*, 急行) to Hannō (飯能) Station, and change there to a local train bound for Seibu-Chichibu. Express trains take a little longer. In either case, the fare is ¥460.

Don't be alarmed when the train appears to leave Hannō Station in the direction from which it arrived. This is due to an unusual arrangement of the tracks, and the train soon branches off onto another line.

From Higashi-Agano Station to Mt. Tenkaku (50 minutes)

Leave the station, turn right, and follow the gravel path across the railway line to a bitumen road, where you should turn right again. Bear left at the nearby intersection. Very soon you will see a small lane marked "Mt. Tenkaku, Mt. Ōtaka access" (天覚山 大高山入口) veering off to the right. Proceed along this lane, which soon becomes a wide path leading past a small cemetery.

About 10 minutes from the station, continue straight through the junction near a road. A sign here that indicates "direction of Mt. Tenkaku" (天覚山方面) is painted on a tree, as are many other signs along this route. In spring, white *utsugi* (one of several kinds

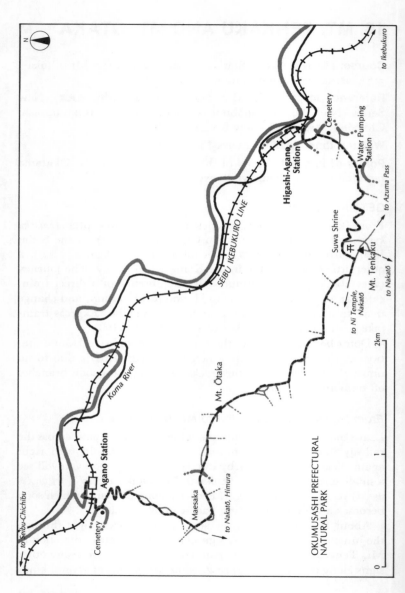

OKUMUSASHI PREFECTURAL
NATURAL PARK

of deutzia common to the area), white-and-yellow daisies, yellow *nigana* (*Ixeris dentata*), and purple thistle flowers bloom beside the trail. There are also several kinds of strawberry, including *hebiichigo* (Indian strawberry). After about 7 minutes, you pass a water pumping station, which is also near a bend in the mountain road, and walk uphill to the right of the water channel. The forest to the left has been cleared—ignore the path that soon branches off in that direction.

The trail becomes narrower and steeper as it climbs to the heavily forested summit of Mt. Tenkaku (天覚山頂), but you should reach there in 30 minutes or so. This slope has white *gakuutsugi* (hydrangea) and *futarishizuka* (*Chloranthus serratus*), and purple-and-white *shaga* (fringed iris) flowers in spring. Just below the top is the small Suwa Shrine, dedicated to the god Daimyōjin. The path to the left of the shrine leads to a first junction, where the left-hand path goes to Azuma Pass (東峠), and then to a second, with a path to Nakatō (中藤). However, take the right-hand path behind the shrine to another junction about 50 meters away. To the right is the continuation of the path to Mt. Ōtaka, but first go left up to the relatively low, 445-meter summit of Mt. Tenkaku (*Tenkaku-san*), though the view may be obscured by the forest.

From Mt. Tenkaku to Mt. Ōtaka (1 hour 15 minutes)

Return to the previous junction and pass straight through, downhill. After 5 minutes, bear right, away from Ni Temple (*Nittera*, 新寺) and Nakatō (中藤) and toward Mt. Ōtaka (大高山). Although the forest this ridge trail passes through, as it bobs up and down across a series of small peaks, is mostly planted, much of this is old, and, with the patches of native forest, is home to various birds and butterflies.

Ignore the many minor paths branching off down other ridges and spurs, and follow the signs for Mt. Ōtaka, Maesaka (前坂), and Agano Station (吾野駅). Note also that in several places the trail divides into left and right arms that soon rejoin; these are usually marked with the symbol ⌀ or the characters 左の道も右の道も同じ, which mean "the left and right tracks are the same."

In addition to ferns, spring wildflowers (including violets, yellow daisies and small white roses), and the strawberries already mentioned, there are delicious amber *momijiichigo* raspberries in summer, the latter usually near cleared areas.

This rugged section of the path, which in one place has a rope "railing," takes you over or around several peaks, including one rocky crag with good views to the right, which is a good place for lunch. Make sure you leave in the direction marked for Mt. Ōtaka.

About 1 hour 10 minutes after passing the turnoff to Ni Temple and Nakatō, you should reach the top of Mt. Ōtaka (*Ōtakayama*). A signboard here declares this peak to be 493 meters above sea level. There are reasonably good views of the Naguri area and Okutama mountains to the left.

From Mt. Ōtaka to Agano Station (1 hour 10 minutes)

Descend the other side of the summit in the direction of Maesaka and Agano Station (前坂 吾野駅方面). Follow similar signs to a forest road at a pass some 20–25 minutes away. Along this road are many spring wildflowers, including yellow *hahakogusa* (cotton- or cudweed) and white *shirotsumekusa* (Dutch clover).

Continue the walk by climbing the steps, again signposted for Maesaka and Agano Station, on the opposite side of the road. This and subsequent areas have more spring wildflowers, including purple *koajisai* (hydrangea with clusters of small flowers). Turn right toward Agano Station (吾野駅) at the intersection at Maesaka 15 minutes later. The path to the left leads to Nakatō and Himura (中藤 飛村), while that straight on is a mountain path going in the general direction of the temple of Nenogongen (a walk to which is also described in the Okumusashi section).

The trail eventually zigzags down through plantations to Agano Town, emerging at a road next to a cemetery 25–30 minutes later. Walk the short distance down this road to a signposted dirt path on the right, which leads to a pedestrian tunnel under the railway line. On the other side, take the right-hand steps up to the road to Agano Station, which is about 50 meters away.

Return to Ikebukuro on the trains described in the "Getting There" section for this walk. The fare is ¥490, and the trip will take a few minutes longer than the outward journey.

19. NENOGONGEN AND TAKE TEMPLE – M

Course: Agano Station → Nenogongen → Take Temple → Kodono Town → (by bus) → Hannō Station

Reference map: Nitchi Map No. 1 (Okumusashi, 奥武蔵), New Series No. 20; or Shōbunsha Map No. 25 (Okumusashi Chichibu, 奥武蔵 秩父), New Series No. 25.

Walking time: About 3 hours 30 minutes.

Points of interest: Mountain forests, superb views of surrounding ranges, the bell at the temple of Nenogongen, Take Temple.

GETTING THERE

From Ikebukuro Station, it is best to take a rapid express (*kaisoku kyūkō*, 快速特急) bound for Seibu-Chichibu (西武秩父) on the Seibu Ikebukuro Line (西武池袋線). Alight at Agano (吾野) Station, after a ride of about 1 hour 10 minutes. If there is no direct train for some time, catch an express (kyūkō, 急行) to Hannō (飯能) Station, and change there to a local train bound for Seibu-Chichibu. Express trains take a little longer. In either case, the journey costs ¥490.

Don't be alarmed when the train appears to leave Hannō Station in the direction from which it arrived. This is due to the unusual arrangement of the tracks, and the train soon branches off onto another line.

From Agano Station to Nenogongen (1 hour 30 minutes)

Leave by the only exit at Agano Station and walk down the bitumen road to the left, in the same direction that the train was traveling. After about 50 meters, the road curves around and a temple lies straight ahead. At the curve, ignore the sign to Nenogongen (子の権現) on the right, and instead go up the steps on the left, following the dirt path next to the railway line. Continue on this path down to the main road. There, turn left immediately onto the bitumen road that leads up to a quarry on the opposite side of the railway. Before the quarry, you will cross a bridge over the railway tracks. Take the small dirt road to the right, just after the bridge—a sign here points to Nenogongen. No more than 10–15 minutes should have elapsed since you left the station.

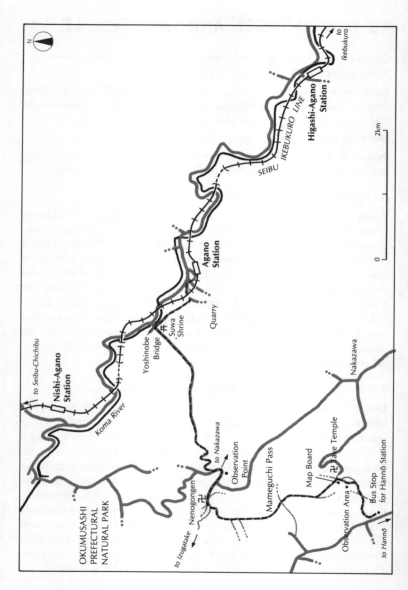

After a couple of minutes, the dirt road becomes a pleasant little path that wanders past some houses and around the side of a hill. Some 5 minutes later, you pass through a small forest known for a particular variety of *rindō* (gentian) and then come back onto bitumen as you reach a small town and Suwa Shrine. You will soon come to an intersection next to a bridge (called *Yoshi-nobebashi*, 芳延橋), with the road to the right leading across the bridge to the main highway. Turn left and follow the bitumen road uphill. The road gradually becomes steeper, following the course of a small stream into the mountains, but it is well signposted for Nenogongen. Some 30 minutes after turning at the intersection, the road becomes dirt, and 10 minutes later you should encounter a small bridge with traditional curved railings. This is the start of the path to Nenogongen.

Half an hour of hard climbing through forests that in late summer and early autumn are alive with the sound of *aburazemi* and *niiniizemi* (cicadas) and are dotted with *inutade* (pink-beaded knotgrass) will bring you to a road with a sign indicating Nishi-Agano Station (西吾野駅) to the right. Go left along the road, which leads to the Nenogongen temple complex. Prior to reaching there, however, on the left you pass the start of a small path (marked as "difficult") to Nakazawa (中沢) and then pass through a large roofed car park. Just before some small noodle and souvenir stands is an observation area on a peak to the left. The view from here is quite extensive, and in winter the surrounding snow-covered ranges are spectacular. In autumn, the *momiji* (Japanese maple) leaves of various shades of red, yellow, and orange adorn this point.

The temple lies past a road (to Nakazawa), an old tree of unusually large girth, the shops mentioned, and two giants guarding the entrance. Above and behind the temple, which is quite new and of limited interest, is a bell platform. You can experience the fine resonance of this giant bell by swinging the large wooden beam—the sound continues for several minutes after it has been struck. A good place for lunch!

From Nenogongen to Take Temple (1 hour)

To proceed to Take Temple (*Takedera*, 竹寺), go under the covered

Shimenawa (sacred straw festoon) entrance at Take Temple.

passageway with the large clock, to the left of Nenogongen's temple office. Between some buildings, you will see a sign pointing along the dirt road to Take Temple that you must take. Ignore the path leading downhill to the left that appears after a minute or so. Similarly ignore the two roads to the right at one junction a little farther on. From here, it is mainly a matter of staying on the main path, which runs through Okumusashi Prefectural Natural Park to Take Temple.

About 5 minutes after leaving the temple, you come to some steps at a signposted junction that head up to the right to Izugatake (伊豆ヶ岳). Ignore this path and continue straight on, which is indicated as the direction for Take Temple and Mt. Neno (*Neno-san*, 子ノ山). The path wanders through minor junctions, and around and up and down a few peaks. Simply follow the signs for Take Temple, and in 30–40 minutes you will reach Mameguchi Pass (豆口峠). A small A-frame shelter is perched on the ridge here, with tracks sloping down either side. The path to the left meets the road to Nakazawa, and the one to the right leads to the main road, which is served by a bus to Hannō Station (飯能駅). However, to see Take Temple continue straight on.

Some 10–15 minutes later, at a signposted junction, a path veers off to the right. Keep to the left, and in less than 10 minutes you reach a junction with an adjacent hiking map board, and Take Temple and its associated buildings in front of you. The temple is graced with beautiful bamboo flanking its main path on the side opposite to your approach. It is peaceful place to relax, especially by the pond.

The official name of the temple is very long, apparently too long for the local people, who just call it Takedera (*take* means "bamboo"). If you fancy having a vegetarian lunch complete with *sansai* (mountain vegetables) in the temple dining hall, reservations can be made for a few occasions during spring and autumn by telephoning the temple in Japanese at (04297)7-0108. The meal, which costs ¥5,000, is served in bamboo utensils and is accompanied by a detailed explanation of the food in Japanese by one of the priests.

There is a road leading down from the temple to Nakazawa (中沢), from where a bus goes to Hannō Station (40 minutes), so this is an alternative way of returning to Tokyo.

From Take Temple to Kodono (1 hour)

To complete the walk, return to the map board and take the uphill path. Almost immediately, there is a signposted fork. Go right, uphill, to "Kodono via the Bell Tower" (鐘つき堂を経て小殿), thus ignoring the path marked 名栗小殿 35分. In 10 minutes, you reach an observation area on top of a small peak. Bamboo pointers here indicate the directions of various local features including a dam, and you can clearly see a pagoda and a huge white *torii kannon* figure (actually one large statue with two smaller statues), viewed from the side. There is another bell here.

Continue down the path on the other side, to the left of the observation area. A sign marked "40-minute shortcut to Naguri and Kodono" (名栗小殿近道 40分) is at the start of the path. This area has small yellow (*yakushisō* hawk's beard) flowers in autumn. Ignore the track to the left (back to Take Temple) at the junction soon after, and keep going downhill, staying on the main path. Part of the face of this hill has been completely cleared of trees, leaving a dangerous drop next to the path, so be careful. However, the lack of trees at this point does allow autumn colors on the hills on the opposite side of the valley to be enjoyed. The path then zigzags, and 30–40 minutes after leaving the observation area, you should reach the main road, where you go left.

The stop for the bus to Hannō Station is about 100 meters down the road. The trip takes 50 minutes and costs ¥580. The train fare from Hannō Station to Ikebukuro Station is ¥370.

20. BŌ PEAK ———————————————————— D

Course: Hannō Station (by bus) → Kawamata → Gonjiri Pass → Bō Peak → Gonjiri Pass → Mt. Kuro → Nasaka Pass → Kawai Station

Reference map: Nitchi Map No. 1 (Okumusashi, 奥武蔵), New Series No. 20; or Shōbunsha Map No. 24 (Okutama, 奥武蔵 秩父), New Series No. 24.

Walking time: About 4 hours 45 minutes.

Points of interest: Good views of the Okumusashi and Okutama mountains, and wildflowers, especially in spring.

GETTING THERE

From Ikebukuro Station, take an express (*kyūkō*, 急行) or a rapid express train (*kaisoku kyūkō*, 快速特急) bound for Hannō (飯能) Station or Seibu-Chichibu (西武秩父) Station on the Seibu Ikebukuro Line (西武池袋線), and get off at Hannō Station. The journey takes 45–50 minutes and costs ¥370.

Leave the station by the only exit, walk straight ahead to Bus Stand No. 2, and take a No. 1 bus bound for Yunosawa (湯の沢). The road winds through the Naguri River valley, and in spring you should be able to see *mitsubatsutsuji* (three-leafed azalea), *ume* (plum), and *boke* (Japanese quince) flowers along the way. Get off after about 45 minutes at Kawamata (河又) Bus Stop. The fare is ¥520.

From Kawamata to Bō Peak (2 hours)

Walk in the direction the bus was traveling past a map board and a sign for Arima Dam and Bō Peak (有間ダム 棒ノ嶺), and then veer left across a bridge, away from the main road. A little farther on, at a corner, is another map board and signs indicating alternative routes to Bō Peak that both begin as roads. Take the road to the left, marked "Bō Peak Ridge Trail" (棒ノ嶺尾根道). The right-hand track goes via Arima Dam.

Pass by a bridge that leads back toward the main road and within a minute you will see another bridge to the left that crosses the stream (Arima River) running beside the road you are on. Cross this bridge to where there are a few houses, and turn left and then, within a few meters, right, toward Bō Peak as indicated on the signs. (Note that although the path to Bō Peak is very well indicated, because of the different syllabaries of Japanese, the existence of both old and simplified Chinese characters, and the additional complication that this mountain has more than one name, the signs for Bō Peak (*Bō-no-mine*) may be written as 棒ノ嶺 or 棒の峰, as some combination of these, or even as 棒ノ折山.)

The dirt path skirts a family cemetery plot and then quickly leads up into cedar and cyprus forest. Ignore paths branching off to the left and then right soon after, and follow the signs. In the absence of signs, stay on the main trail. The path is a steep but pleasant climb up the ridge. About 35 minutes from the bus stop is a path to the left marked "to Imourami" (至芋浦美), but continue straight through, eventually into deciduous forest with *sasa* (dwarf bamboo) on the sides of the trail.

Rocky Kawamata Ridge is renowned for its beautiful light pink *iwauchiwa* (shortia) flowers in mid- to late April. The flowering *asebi* (Japanese andromeda), *mansaku* (Japanese witch hazel), *tsunohashibami* (another type of hazel) and *aburachan* (*Parabenzoin praecox*) trees are common here, too. In addition, there are good views of Arima Dam along this section.

After 50 minutes or so, you reach Iwatakeishi, a rock that stands several meters high in the middle of the path. Just beyond the rock are signposted paths on the left and right. To the left is "Tōgiiri Forest Road" (トウギイリ林道へ) (the local meaning of the *iri* in the name is "swamp"). This is also the direction for Naguri, where there is a radium spring. The path to the right, marked "Shiraya Valley mountain climbing access" (白谷沢登山口), passes Shirokujaku Waterfall and a gorge. However, continue straight through this junction in the direction of Gonjiri Pass and Bō Peak (ゴンジリ峠 棒ノ嶺). After 25 minutes you reach the pass, with paths to the left and right and excellent views of the ranges straight ahead.

From here, go right toward "Bō Peak, Hyakkenjaya" (棒の嶺 百軒茶屋), the first of which is only 10 minutes away. Bō Peak stands 976 meters high, with views to the north and east (the

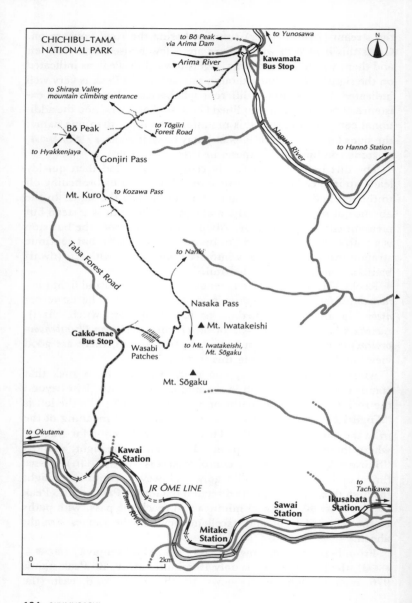

CHICHIBU–TAMA
NATIONAL PARK

to Bō Peak
via Arima Dam

to Yunosawa

Arima River

Kawamata
Bus Stop

to Shiraya Valley
mountain climbing entrance

to Tōgiiri
Forest Road

Nagura River

to Hannō Station

Bō Peak

to Hyakkenjaya

Gonjiri Pass

Mt. Kuro

to Kozawa Pass

Taba Forest Road

to Nariki

Nasaka Pass

▲ Mt. Iwatakeishi

Gakkō-mae
Bus Stop

Wasabi
Patches

to Mt. Iwatakeishi,
Mt. Sōgaku

▲
Mt. Sōgaku

to Okutama

Kawai
Station

JR ŌME LINE

to
Tachikawa

Ikusabata
Station

Sawai
Station

Mitake
Station

Tama River

0   1   2km

N

Arima Dam viewed from Kawamata Ridge.

Okumusashi and Okuchichibu areas) as a result of the forest being cleared; Okutama is on the other side and can't be seen. The many wildflowers, including *yamatsutsuji* (mountain azalea), on the surrounding slopes are another attraction of this peak, making it a good place to have lunch, unless you want to return to Gonjiri Pass first.

Note that, as an alternative, this walk can be completed by taking the path from the summit to the left, toward Hyakkenjaya, down to the Taba Forest Road (丹波林道), which takes about 40 minutes. There you can catch a bus or walk down the valley past several camp sites to Kawai Station (about 1 hour 10 minutes).

From Bō Peak to Kawai Station (2 hours 45 minutes)

Return to Gonjiri Pass, which takes about 5 minutes and continue straight through the junction there, toward Mt. Kuro and Mt. Iwatakeishi (黒山 岩茸石山). This route follows a ridge that descends steeply.

After 15–20 minutes, you reach the summit of Mt. Kuro (*Kuroyama*, 黒山, known locally as *Kuroiwa*). The path straight ahead leads to Kozawa Pass (小沢峠), but turn right toward Mt. Iwatakeishi (岩茸石山) and Mt. Sōgaku (惣岳山). Go straight through the small signposted junction shortly after, and ignore any small tracks that veer off later—just follow the signs for Mt. Iwatakeishi and Mt. Sōgaku. This area has many interesting plants and fungi, and at one point on the ridge the surrounding trees have been cleared, allowing good views of the valley. The ensuing native forest is a good place to spot small birds. From here the trail meanders up and down until you reach Nasaka Pass.

Just over an hour after leaving Mt. Kuro, at a T-junction where the path to the left leads to Nariki (成木), turn right toward Mt. Iwatakeishi and Mt. Sōgaku. Some 10–15 minutes later, at Nasaka Pass (名坂峠) just before Mt. Iwatakeishi, turn hard right toward Ōtaba and Kawai Station (大丹波 川井駅). This track initially zigzags down a slope and is steep and badly eroded, so care is needed. Later, it follows a rocky ridge through cedar plantations to a stream and then over a series of bridges. Beside this stream *wasabi* (Japanese horseradish) plants, which have small white flowers in May, are cultivated in stony "fields" surrounded by rock walls. Stay on the main path, toward Ōtaba and Kawai Station.

In 40–45 minutes, after passing a stand of bamboo and rows of logs on which *shiitake* mushrooms are grown, the path becomes a small lane running through a pretty farming hamlet and soon meets a road. Kawai Station is to the left, some 30 minutes walk away. If you prefer to take a bus, Gakkō-mae Bus Stop is just a few meters to your right. The fare is ¥140 for the 5-minute ride.

If you walk, you can enter the station by going up the small road to the left that runs, from the main road reached after about 25 minutes, under the railway line and uphill beside the station. If the ticket office is closed, obtain a ticket by pressing the button on the machine at the station entrance, and pay on the train or at your destination (the fare to Shinjuku is ¥930). There is only a single line here, so make sure you get on a train going to the left as you face the tracks. The journey to Tachikawa takes 55 minutes. Change there for a Chūō Line (中央線) rapid service train (*kaisoku*, 快速) or special rapid service train (*tokubetsu kaisoku*, 特別快速) to Shinjuku (38 and 27 minutes, respectively).

HAKONE

21. MYŌJŌ PEAK ─────────── M

Course: Odawara Station (by bus) → Miyaginobashi → Myōjō Peak → Mt. Matsuo → Tō Peak → Amida Temple → Hakone-Yumoto Station

Reference map: Nitchi Map No. 7 (Hakone, 箱根), New Series No. 26; or Shōbunsha New Series Map No. 19 (Hakone, 箱根).

Walking time: About 4 hours.

Points of interest: Valley views, the annual Daimonjiyaki Festival on the side of Myōjō Peak, spring wildflowers, Amida Temple.

GETTING THERE

From Shinjuku Station, take an Odakyū Line (小田急線) express (*kyūkō,* 急行) from Platform 4 or 5 to Odawara (小田原) Station. As the Odakyū Line branches at Sagami-Ōno (相模大野) Station, make sure you are on a train bound for Odawara or Hakone-Yumoto (箱根湯本), and *not* Enoshima (江ノ島). Also, some trains divide at Sagami-Ōno, with the front and the rear having different destinations, in which case you should board one of the front carriages. The trip takes 1 hour 25–40 minutes and costs ¥630.

A slightly faster (1 hour 10–15 minutes) and much more comfortable means of getting to Odawara is by the limited express (*tokkyū,* 特急) called the "Romance Car" from Platform 2 or 3 on the same line. Note, however, that this train is less frequent, often requires booking in advance, and costs an additional ¥620.

At Odawara Station, pass through the central Odakyū ticket barrier but retain your ticket, as you are still within the JR station. Turn left and walk along the passageway to the JR exit. Go down the steps just outside that lead below to a shopping mall. At the bottom, slightly to the left, are steps marked バスのりば 1-8 (Bus Stands Nos. 1–8). Climb these and go to Bus Stand No. 4. There, catch a No. 2 bus, and get off at Miyaginobashi (宮城野橋). The

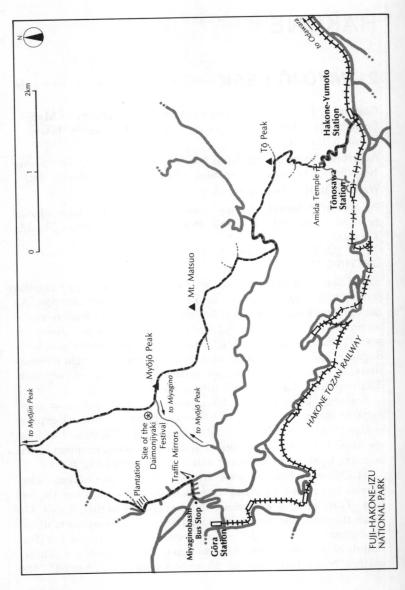

FUJI-HAKONE-IZU
NATIONAL PARK

journey up the winding mountain road lasts 35–40 minutes, and the fare is ¥650.

From Miyaginobashi to Myōjō Peak (1 hour 50 minutes)

Cross the bridge next to the bus stop, and immediately turn right. Within 5 minutes you reach a T-junction with two traffic mirrors. To begin the walk, you can go in either direction, but the left branch, described here, takes about 30–40 minutes longer.

If you want to take the alternative route, follow the right-hand road for a few minutes to an intersection, turn left, and then take the road marked for Myōjō Peak (明星ヶ岳) that veers uphill to the left a little further on. *Gamazumi* (dockmackie) trees can be seen along the left side of the road just before this fork.

Assuming, however, that you go left at the T-junction, after walking for approximately 10 minutes you will see, between a small cedar plantation and another road, a map board and a path that leads up the mountain to your right. This rocky trail runs next to a stone wall and a few houses and is quite steep. In places, mostly on the left, you find *tsunohashibami* (a kind of hazel), while later on the right are stands of bamboo. Stay on the main path here.

On reaching the beginning of a road that leads off to the left, continue straight ahead in the direction marked "Myōjin Peak" (明神ヶ岳). Soon after, the track enters dense bamboo forest with abundant bird life. At times the bamboo forms an arch over the

Arch of bamboo on the climb to Myōjō Peak.

path. Subsequently, the trail passes into deciduous forest and crosses a stream bed. It then runs between this and a second nearby rocky bed (which joins the first a little downhill), finally crossing the second stream bed. Large-leafed *sasa* (dwarf bamboo) and rocks of volcanic origin characterize the ensuing area. You should reach the top of the ridge 50–60 minutes after leaving the map board.

When you get to the nearby junction, turn right toward Myōjō Peak (明星ヶ岳). (The track to the left ascends Myōjin Peak.) From here, the trail is quite easy, bobbing up and down across a series of wide, cleared ridges that stretch for some kilometers, with superb views of the surrounding valleys. Anywhere along this section is good for a lunch stop.

Some 35–40 minutes along this ridge, a path to Miyagino (宮城野) branches off to the right—this is the other end of the alternative trail mentioned before. Consequently, ignore this path and continue straight ahead, in the direction of Tō Peak (塔ヶ峰).

Less than 5 minutes away is the 924-meter-high summit of Myōjō Peak (*Myōjōgatake*), where there is a miniature shrine surrounded by stone figures and a stone tablet. The summit is relatively flat and the overgrown shrine overlooks a small clearing on the left.

Of interest here is the mountain slope used for the Daimonjiyaki Festival, that is, the burning of the Chinese character 大 (dai), meaning "large" or "great" (the ideograph of a man standing with his arms stretched out wide). For this reason, Myōjō Peak is also know as Mt. Daimonji. Each year, on August 16, huge torches in an arrangement of the three strokes of this character measuring 162, 108, and 81 meters, are set alight. The actual site of the bonfire is a little way down the path to Miyagino that you just passed, on the right as you descend.

From Myōjō Peak to Hakone-Yumoto Station (2 hours 10 minutes)

Continuing toward Mt. Matsuo, the path descends past another stone tablet before beginning to rise again. Wildflowers, especially in spring, and many small birds are common here. Ignore any tracks leading off and continue straight ahead, toward Tō Peak.

About 25 minutes from Myōjō Peak, the path skirts the top of

Mt. Matsuo (*Matsuoyama*, 松尾山), and then drops again before rising through a plantation. Some 10 minutes later, the trail swings hard right and goes directly and very steeply downhill. There is no signpost here, so be sure not to continue straight on. You pass a tall electricity pylon on your descent to a gravel road 15 minutes away. There, follow the road downhill in the direction of Tō Peak as signposted. On clear days, you can see across Sagami Bay to the Miura Peninsula, and many flowering hydrangeas grow by the roadside. Approximately 15 minutes down this road is a path and an adjacent sign indicating Tō Peak (*Tō-no-mine*) to the right.

Some 10–15 minutes along this path is the summit and a fork. The board here tells how a pagoda containing remains of the Buddha, enshrined by the great Indian king Ashoka, were found in a rock cave at Amida Temple farther down the hill. For this reason, the mountain was called Tō (Pagoda) Peak. The summit itself was the site of a castle of Odawara's Hōjō clan.

Turn right at this fork, in the direction of Amida Temple and Tōnosawa (阿弥陀寺 塔之沢). The trail zigzags downhill through forest with *aoki* (a red-berried Japanese laurel), *yamazakura* (wild cherry), *momi* (fir), *momiji* (Japanese maple) and *kaede* (another type of maple) trees and, eventually, a bamboo stand. After 30 minutes or so, you arrive at the rear of Amida Temple. With its thatched roof and antiquated appearance, it is an attractive place, even when the surrounding pink, purple, and blue hydrangeas and the many other flowers are not in bloom.

Blossoms adorn the grounds of Amida Temple.

Walk past the statues at the front of the temple and down the stone steps next to the concrete road. Some 5 minutes along this path is an intersection: to the right, directly downhill, is Tōno-sawa (塔之沢); to the left, via the small road, is Yumoto (湯本).

If you decide to go to Tōnosawa Station, you can take the Hakone Tozan Railway (箱根登山鉄道), a "zigzag" train with lots of switchbacks. To do so, turn left at the junction of the stone steps after 6 or 7 minutes, and then right several minutes later (just before the path ends at a road), along a small dirt track that winds around the edge of some houses. Wild strawberries and flowers can be found here in season. Tōnosawa Station is a few minutes away, at the bottom of a small slope. You can change to the Odakyū Line to return to Shinjuku at either Hakone-Yumoto Station or Odawara Station. The respective fares for these relatively short journeys are ¥100 and ¥270. If the station is unmanned, buy your ticket on the train or pay the total at your destination.

If you don't want to go to Tōnosawa Station but wish to complete the main walk at Hakone-Yumoto Station (箱根湯本駅), take the small concrete road downhill in the direction of Yumoto, veering left onto the larger road that leads further downhill and, after some 15–20 minutes, under the railway line. The station is then 100 meters farther on to your left. The express to Shinjuku takes approximately 1 hour 55 minutes and costs ¥870. Limited express "Romance Cars" also leave from this station (1 hour 25–35 minutes and an additional ¥620).

CHICHIBU

22. MT. HAPPU ──────────────────────────── E

Course: Minano Station (by bus) → Mukumiyabashi → Mt. Happu → Fudatate Pass → Suisen Temple → Fudasho-mae (by bus) → Minano Station

Reference map: Minano (皆野) 1:25,000 Sheet Map.

Walking time: About 2 hours.

Points of interest: Spring wildflowers, excellent views of the surrounding plains and foothills, Suisen Temple.

GETTING THERE

From Ikebukuro Station, take a Seibu Ikebukuro Line (西武池袋線) rapid express train (*kaisoku kyūkō,* 快速急行) to Seibu-Chichibu (西武秩父) Station. This costs ¥640 for the journey of 1 hour 35 minutes. Alternatively, take an express (*kyūkō,* 急行) to Hannō (飯能) Station and transfer to a train for Seibu-Chichibu. A third possibility is the faster (15 minutes less than the rapid express) and more comfortable "Red Arrow" limited express (*tokkyū,* 特急) on the same line. Note, however, that the latter is less frequent, is often fully booked, and has a ¥570 surcharge.

At Seibu-Chichibu Station, turn left as you come out, walk past the souvenir shops, and follow the lane to the left, indicated by the sign saying, "Chichibu Railway Ohanabatake Station" (秩父鉄道御花畑駅), around to a road that crosses the railway line. Cross the tracks and immediately turn right, thus following them via a small lane to Ohanabatake Station (御花畑駅) on the Chichibu Railway Line (秩父鉄道). There, catch any train in the direction of Yorii (寄居) to Minano (皆野) Station (¥270, 15 minutes).

Leave Minano Station by its only exit, walk down the road straight ahead to the intersection and turn left. The bus terminus is 50–100 meters farther on your right, on a corner with a high tower. Catch a Seibu bus bound for Kami-Yoshida (上吉田), and get off at Mukumiyabashi (椋宮橋). The bus fare is ¥170, and the

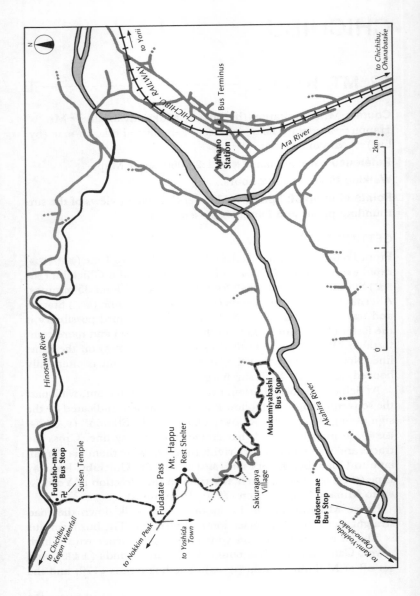

Valley of the Akahira and Ara rivers.

trip takes only 10 minutes. As these buses are not frequent, it may be necessary instead to take an Ogano-shako (小鹿野車庫)-bound bus to Batōsen-mae (馬頭尊前) (¥180, 10–15 minutes), and walk for about 30 minutes in the direction opposite to that of the bus, to Mukumiyabashi Bus Stop.

If the times of both buses are inconvenient, walk to Mukumiyabashi by following the same road you took to reach the bus terminus back past the small road to the station and across the river. There, turn right, cross another river, turn hard left, and continue along this road. It will take about 50 minutes to get to Mukumiyabashi.

From Mukumiyabashi to Mt. Happu (1 hour 20 minutes)

Close to the bus stop is a bridge that crosses a small stream. Follow the nearby concrete road, marked "Mt. Happu hiking course" (破風山 ハイキングコース), which leads uphill beyond houses next to the stream. Stay on this road. The pleasant climb takes you past a kiln and through a mix of farms, plantations, and native forest. Spinach, spring onions, and Japanese radish are among the vegetables grown here. Spring wildflowers that flourish beside this road include various violets, purple and mauve *kakidōshi* (ground ivy), and *hotokenoza* (henbit or bee nettle). In addition, there are good views (mainly to the left and rear) that open out as you get higher.

After about 30 minutes, just before the village of Sakuragaya, you should see a rocky path that veers uphill to the right. A sign here identifies this as the old way to Mt. Happu (破風山旧道). Follow this route between farms with cows and chickens and a few old houses, some with thatched roofs, turning to the right at the fork and then keeping left at the sign marked "Mt. Happu to the left" (左破風山に至る).

Within 10 minutes from its start, the path rejoins the concrete road. Cross the road and ascend via the small concrete lane on the opposite side. Past the nearby house, the lane becomes a dirt path again. Ignoring the many tracks that lead off, follow this path for 6 minutes or so, past gravestones and through forest consisting of a variety of fruit and flowering cherry trees and bamboo, back to the road, on both sides of which are several rows of logs for the cultivation of mushrooms.

The trail continues to the left about 50 meters farther uphill. Again stay on the main path. There are more spring wildflowers here: *tōdaigusa* (euphorbia) clusters, yellow spurs of *miyamakikeman* (corydalis), white *momijiichigo* (maple-leaf raspberry) and yellow-green *yabusanzashi* (thicket hawthorn or May tree) among them, as well as a wealth of birds and butterflies.

Approximately 15 minutes later, at the end of a dirt road, take the uphill path marked "Mt. Happu summit" (破風山頂), and 5 minutes later turn right toward "Mt. Happu summit via wooden shelter" (木憩舎を経て破風山頂へ). A further 5 minutes on is a rest shelter, from which a narrow ridge leads to the summit just a few minutes away.

Although, at 627 meters, Mt. Happu (*Happu-san*) is not one of the taller peaks of the area, it has a spectacular 360° panoramic view of the mountain ranges to the west and the rice plains of the Ara and Akahira River valleys, separated by rolling hills, to the east. It is harder to imagine a better place for lunch.

From Mt. Happu to Fudasho-mae (40 minutes)

Proceed down the steep ridge on the other side of the summit, going straight through the signposted junction after five minutes. Turn right at Fudatate Pass 5 minutes later, toward Hinosawa and Suisen Temple, as indicated on the sign (日野沢 水潜寺に至る). To the left is Yoshida Town, and straight ahead is a rocky crag named Nokkim Peak.

The trail zigzags down a rocky valley, eventually paralleling a stream that it crosses several times by way of log bridges. Although the forest here is mostly planted, there are also some wildflowers and flowers of deciduous trees in spring, among them yellow-green "bells" of *kibushi* (*Stachyurus praecox*). You should reach the temple in 25–30 minutes. Suisen Temple (*Suisen-ji*, 水潜寺) is attractively nestled in the valley, and has beside it a cave containing stone Buddhist figures. The approach to the temple is lined with small statues.

Walk the 100 meters or so down the lane from the temple to the main road, where the tributary flowing beside the temple runs into the larger Hinosawa River. To the left is a gift shop that sells mushroom-flavored *sembei* (Japanese rice crackers); *yamakonnyaku* (mountain devil's tongue root) is another local specialty. In this charming village, some houses are situated right on the edge of the river, while others perch high on the mountain side. Another attraction is Chichibu Kegon Waterfall, with a 20–meter drop, which is 10 minutes upstream. Not far from the waterfall is a bus stop.

Immediately on your right is Fudasho-mae (札所前) Bus Stop. Note that the last bus leaves here at about 4:50 P.M. The fare to Minano Station is ¥180, and the journey takes approximately 15 minutes. Return to Ikebukuro Station by following in reverse the instructions in the "Getting There" section for this walk.

NIKKŌ

23. SENJŌ FIELD ———————————— E

Course: Tōbu-Nikkō Station (by bus) → Kohan-mae → Senjō
Field → Shōbugahama (by bus) → Tōbu-Nikkō Station

Reference map: Nitchi Map No. 8 (Okunikkō, Okukinu, 奥日光 奥
鬼怒), New Series No. 30; or Shōbunsha Map No. 43 (Nikkō, 日光),
New Series No. 31.

Walking time: About 2 hours 40 minutes.

Points of interest: A lakeside walk, native forest and marsh trails,
spring alpine wildflowers, various birds and animals.

GETTING THERE

At Asakusa Station, board a Tōbu Line (東武線) rapid service train
(*kaisoku*, 快速) bound for Tōbu-Nikkō (東武日光) Station. These
trains frequently separate at Shimo-Imaichi (下今市) Station, with
the rear carriages going to Kinugawa (鬼怒川). Thus, be sure to get
in one of the front two carriages, and get off at the terminus. The
trip takes approximately 2 hours 10 minutes and costs ¥1,140.
Another possibility is the faster (about 1 hour 45 minutes) and
more comfortable limited express (*tokkyū*, 特急), which has reserved
seating and a ¥1,140 surcharge. Rapid service trains and limited
expresses both leave about once an hour, usually on or just after
the hour.

From the exit of Tobū-Nikkō Station, walk straight ahead to
Bus Stand No. 1, catch a bus for Yumoto Spa (*Yumoto onsen*, 湯元温
泉), and get off at Kohan-mae (湖畔前) on the side of Lake Yu and
one stop before the terminus. Even if you miss this stop, you can
walk the few hundred meters back from the terminus. Early on in
the ride, just after turning off the main road through Nikkō, look
out for the sacred Shin Bridge over the Daiya River, and keep an
eye open for monkeys along the way, especially when the bus is
climbing up to Lake Chūzenji. The bus trip lasts about 1 hour 10
minutes, and the fare is ¥1,440.

From Kohan-mae to Senjō Field (about 1 hour 15 minutes)

Walk the few meters to the edge of Lake Yu (*Yu-no-ko*, 湯ノ湖), where there is the beginning of a path on a wooden platform. Follow this path. When it ends, go along the edge of the lake to the continuation of the "Tour of Lake Yu" (湯ノ湖一周) trail. After passing a waterworks, the path meanders above the edge of the lake, one of several in Nikkō National Park and home to various waterbirds including ducks. The diversity of the trees in this area is considerable, with *nezuko* (Japanese arborvitae), *asunaro* (*Hiba arborvitae*), *urajiromomi* (fir), *kometsuga* (Japanese hemlock), *shiuri-zakura* (a kind of cherry), and *buna* (beech) all common.

About 30 minutes from the start, you come to a path marked "Izumigayato Pond" (泉門池) that veers off to the right. The walk described here assumes you take this little-used and particularly enjoyable leafy track, which leads over a forested ridge and down into a narrow valley. Note, however, that it is also possible to reach Senjō Field by continuing along the lakeside path and then turning right at the far end of Lake Yu. Although you will find picnic tables and benches around the edge of the marsh at Senjō Field when you get there, you may find the serenity of this area reason enough to stop for lunch here instead.

The narrow rocky trail mostly hugs the bottom of the right-hand slope—be sure not to follow any paths that climb out of the valley. Deer and foxes frequent this ferny forest with its many tall old trees. The landscape soon changes to one of birch trees surrounded by waist-deep dwarf bamboo. This undergrowth covers the trail in places, making it a little difficult to see, but since it is well worn, it is relatively easy to follow the track beneath.

About 40 minutes from the previous turn-off is a T-junction with a wide path. Turn right onto this wide track. A further 5 minutes on is another junction, near a picnic area beside picturesque Izumigayato Pond, which marks the boundary of the Senjō Field marsh.

From Senjō Field to Shōbugahama (1 hour 25 minutes)

Veer right at this junction toward Aka Marsh (*Aka-numa*, 赤沼) and Ryūzu Waterfall (*Ryūzu-taki*, 竜頭滝), and then keep left toward the

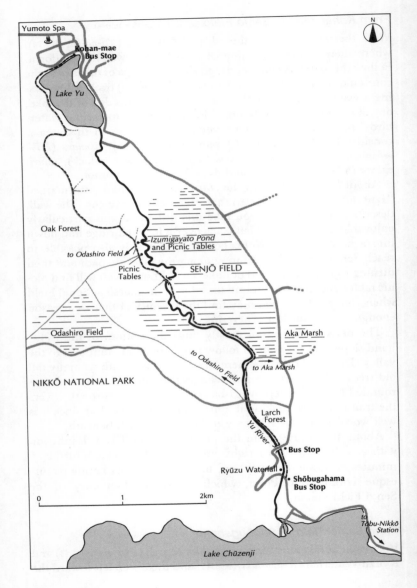

same destinations at the signposted forks shortly after. (The first of the paths to the right leads through *mizunara* [oak] forest to Odashiro Field [小田代原], where *ayame* [blue flag iris], *hakusanfūro* [cranesbill], *kugaisō* [Culver's root], *yamaodamaki* [columbine or aquilegia], and *kurumayuri* [an orange, "wheel-shaped" lily] grow.) Pass more tables and benches near the Yu River (*Yukawa*) and walk along the wooden platforms that extend across the edge of Senjō Field (*Senjōgahara*, 戦場が原) marsh.

The name of the area originates from ancient times, when it was believed that the spirits resided in the mountains. According to the legend, the gods of the peaks of nearby Nantai and Akagi (in Gumma Prefecture) quarreled over who should control the Lake Chūzenji area. In the ensuing battle between the large snakes of Nantai and the centipedes of Akagi, much blood flowed, giving the nearby Aka (Red) Marsh its name. Hence, this swampy tract became known as Senjōgahara (the Battlefield).

At 1,400 meters above sea level, Senjō Field has many alpine trees and wildflowers, particularly in spring, including *ayame* (blue flag iris), *hakusanfūro* (cranesbill), *watasuge* (cotton grass or cotton rush), *tsutsuji* (azalea), and *zumi* (*Malus sieboldii*, a kind of small apple). It also teems with birds most of the year, some of which are *akahara* (brown thrush), *aoji* (black-faced bunting), *enaga* (long-tailed tit), *hōaka* (gray-headed bunting), *kawagarasu* (brown dipper), *kibitaki* (narcissus flycatcher), *kisekirei* (gray wagtail), *kogera* (Japanese pygmy woodpecker), *komadori* (Japanese robin), *kosamebitaki* (brown flycatcher), *magamo* (mallard), *misosazai* (winter wren), *nyūnaisuzume* (russet sparrow), *ōjishigi* (Latham's snipe), *ōruri* (blue-and-white flycatcher), and *nobitaki* (stonechat).

At the junction 10–15 minutes later, turn left and cross the bridge. In the distance are good views of three mountains, Mts. Nantai, Ōmanago, and Komanagao, which are similarly shaped, though progressively farther away. The tallest and closest of these is Mt. Nantai, which was a volcano whose activity had a significant effect on the evolution of this marsh.

Originally, the lava from Mt. Nantai blocked off the Yu River, forming a 30-meter-deep lake. As volcanic debris and silt made the lake shallower, sphagnum moss began to grow out from the shore until it covered the entire water surface, and a marsh was

Mokudō (wooden walkway) across Senjo Field marsh.

Spectacular Ryūzu
Waterfall. (Photo
by Suzanne Quan)

created. Marsh plants such as *watasuge* (cotton grass or cotton rush), *tsurukokemomo* (cranberry or bogberry), *himeshakunage* (Andromeda moorwort) and *mōsengoke* (sundew or dew grass) then proliferated. The marsh is now gradually changing to a grassy field as silt continues to build up due to the accumulation of dead leaves and other material from trees, which increases evaporation and causes the marsh to dry up. Among the new grassland plants establishing themselves on this field are *miyakozasa* (bamboo grass) and *susuki* (pampas grass). In the latter part of this section of the walk you will also see many *shirakaba* (white birch).

Some 35–40 minutes later, just after crossing a bridge, turn right at the T-junction toward Ryūzu Waterfall (竜頭滝). To the left is Aka Marsh (赤沼).

This path shadows the Yu River, whose rapid descent and volcanic rock bed result in a series of small rapids. Trout and salmon make this river and Lake Yu popular fishing spots. Cross over the bitumen road 10 minutes downstream, continuing down the path on the other side. *Karamatsu* (Japanese larch) forest, often found in volcanic regions, dominates to the left.

After 10–15 minutes, near some quite spectacular rapids, you come to another bitumen road. Although it is possible to catch the bus from here, continue down the steps of the wide path on the other side of the road to Ryūzu (Dragon's Head) Waterfall, about 10 minutes away. It is so named because when seen from afar it supposedly looks like a dragon soaring into the sky. The fall cascades vertically some 100 meters over a distance of about 210 meters, and is best viewed from the balcony of the adjacent souvenir shop and restaurant.

To leave the waterfall, walk down to the main road and turn left. Shōbugahama (菖蒲ヶ浜, the name of the nearby beach at Lake Chūzenji) Bus Stop is just 50 meters downhill. Take the bus bound for Nikkō (日光) and get off after about 50 minutes at Tōbu-Nikkō-eki (東武日光駅) Bus Stop in front of Tōbu-Nikkō Station. The fare is ¥1,170.

Return to Asakusa Station by following in reverse the instruction given in the "Getting There" section for this walk. Some trains are not direct, and therefore it may be necessary to change at Shimo-Imaichi Station, about 10 minutes down the line.

CHIBA

24. INBA MARSH ————————————— E

Course: Usui Station → Inba Marsh → Wild Bird Forest → Sakura Station

Reference map: Sakura (佐倉) and Kobayashi (小林) 1:25,000 Sheet Maps.

Walking time: About 3 hours 20 minutes.

Points of interest: A lakeside walk, the birdlife around Inba Marsh, especially in winter, and in the nearby Wild Bird Park.

GETTING THERE

From Platform 3 or 4 of Keisei Ueno Station, take a Keisei Line (京成線) express (*kyūkō*, 急行) bound for Narita (成田) or Narita-kūkō (成田空港) stations, and get off at Usui (臼井) Station (just over 1 hour, ¥570). Alternatively, for the same fare catch a limited express (*tokkyū*, 特急) on the same line to Katsutadai (勝田台), and transfer to an express or local service train for the last part of the journey to Usui (about 55 minutes, excluding connection time). If you use the limited express, take care *not* to get on one of the "Skyliner" limited expresses (which leave from Platforms 1 and 2) —these also go to Narita-kūkō but do not stop along the way. Express trains leave on average about every 25 minutes on weekdays and Saturdays, and about every 40 minutes on Sundays and holidays, with limited expresses departing in between these times.

From Usui Station to the Wild Bird Forest (1 hour 50 minutes)

Leave Usui Station by turning right after passing through the ticket barrier, then right again, and descend via the steps. Walk straight ahead along the small road next to the railway line until after approximately 5 minutes you meet a larger road. Cross this road and go straight down the small lane to another road, where you bear right. Follow this bitumen road around the corner and parallel with the railway again, turning left at the third street, just before an electricity substation, some 10–15 minutes later. In spring, many wildflowers, including purple *hotokenoza* (henbit or bee nettle), *karasunoendō* (a Vicia vetch, literally crow's pea), and *kikeman* (corydalis), mauve *himeodorikosō* (another kind of nettle) and *kakidōshi* (ground ivy or cat's-foot), and yellow *noborogiku* (groundsel), line the sides here and in other places along the trail.

When the road ends, veer to the left and walk across the rice fields to a fenced water channel. A little to the left is a bridge and a break in the fence. Take advantage of these to cross the channel. Next, turn right and follow the line of the fence to a wider channel, and walk beside this by heading left. If the ground surface is too muddy, try one of the paths going in the same direction between paddy fields.

Within 20 minutes of passing the substation, you come to a dirt road and a connecting corrugated galvanized iron bridge that spans the wider water channel. Cross this bridge and climb the embankment. Before you is the western arm of Inba Marsh (*Inba-numa*, 印旛沼), now a lake fringed by reeds and the remains of small wooden retaining structures, and home to various bird species, including wintering ducks, *koajisashi* (little tern), *ōyoshikiri* (great reed warbler), and *yoshigoi* (Chinese little bittern).

To continue in the direction of the Sakura City Wild Bird Forest, turn right and proceed along the top of the embankment that forms the lake boundary. There are usually many kinds of waterbirds in the vegetation at the edge of the water, although you may have to be quiet and patient to get a good look at them. This route takes you past a pumping station and over a bridge, and later past small clumps of *sasa* (dwarf bamboo).

In less than 30 minutes, you arrive at a bitumen road and a large bridge at an inlet of the lake. Turn left over this bridge, walk to the next junction, and then bear hard left along the minor dirt road that parallels a smaller inlet, where there are usually boats moored. At the end of the road, climb the embankment, and make your way next to the low concrete wall. If the path has not been cleared of the tough vegetation that flourishes here, you may have to go partway down the slope facing the lake in order to progress.

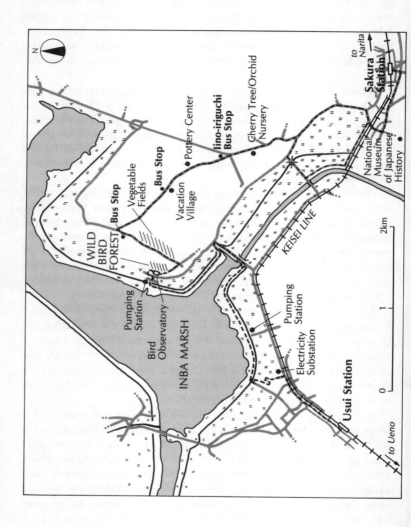

Some 30–40 minutes later (less if the path is clear), you should see a white pumping station located over a small canal about 20 meters to your right. Climb down to this, and use the station surrounds to cross the canal. Take the road 50 meters farther on that branches off toward the nearby escarpment, and turn left at the T-junction shortly after. Within 100 meters a path leads off to the right, next to a map board showing the layout of the Wild Bird Forest (野鳥の森). Springtime white raspberry flowers are common here. Following this path, turn right up the steps at the first intersection. At the top is a semicleared area with many birdhouses mounted on trees. In spring, violets cover the ground and cherry blossoms hang from above. The surrounding woods and fields are frequented by *tsugumi* (dusky thrush), *hakusekirei* (white wagtail), *shijūkara* and *enaga* (great and long-tailed tits), *hōjiro* (Siberian meadow bunting), *onaga* (azure-winged magpie), *mozu* (bull-headed shrike), *kogera* (Japanese pygmy woodpecker), *hototogisu* (little cuckoo), and *hiyodori* (brown-eared bulbul).

There is also a two-story bird observatory, which until recently had a powerful telescope. The observatory can be freely entered at any time. Due to the outstanding lake views and pleasant surroundings, this is an excellent place to stop for lunch.

From the Wild Bird Forest to Sakura Station (1 hour 30 minutes)

To resume the walk, go down the steps on the far side of the clearing, and straight through the junction of paths shortly after. Climb the steps ahead and walk along the bitumen road, past tennis courts, to an intersection. There, turn left, in the signposted direction of Kusabue-no-oka (草ぶえの丘). This rural area has many vegetable fields and greenhouses, some of which are used for *shiitake* (a kind of mushroom) cultivation, and wildflowers on the edges of the road in spring.

Within 25 minutes of leaving the Wild Bird Park, you reach another intersection (just after a bus stop), where you turn right, again towards Kusabue-no-oka. Stay on this road, which passes pine forest on the left, and in about 15 minutes you come to Sakura Natural Vacation Village (佐倉市自然休養村) on the right, a large park that has a collection of old buildings, a camp site, a small railway, bamboo groves, a bird sanctuary, and a coal-fired kiln. Open from 9 A.M. to 5 P.M. (except on Mondays), admission costs ¥300 for adults (¥200 for primary and middle school students, ¥100 for children of 3–5 years). Another stop for the infrequent bus to Sakura Station (佐倉駅) on the Keisei Line is opposite the entrance.

A further 5 minutes brings you to a do-it-yourself pottery center (*Yakimono no sato*, やきものの里) on your left. Less than 10 minutes later, this road merges with the main road. Catching the bus to Sakura Station from Iino-iriguchi (飯野入口) Bus Stop at this corner is convenient (the buses pass here more often than at the other stops mentioned), but if you wish to continue walking or if you have to wait too long for a bus, veer right and follow the main road for 5–10 minutes, past a cherry tree and orchid nursery on the right, to where another road merges from the right. Here you have a choice of routes to the station.

The first route takes about 30 minutes. Go straight on, crossing the railway line, and turning left at the next intersection. The National Museum of Japanese History is on the other side of the road. Turn left at the second set of traffic lights, after passing over a small rise—a sign here in English indicates Keisei-Sakura Station.

The slightly longer but more interesting alternative is to bear hard right at the junction past the nursery, and then left down the small road that runs through paddy fields. Just before a large canal, turn left and follow the dirt path to the railway line. There, head left and walk beside the tracks, crossing them at any road and turning left. At the English-language sign mentioned above, turn left to the station.

To return to Ueno Station, catch either an express or a limited express. These take about 1 hour to 1 hour 10 minutes and cost ¥630. Note that some trains branch off to join the Asakusa Line, so make sure you are on a train bound for Ueno (上野).

BŌSŌ PENINSULA

25. MT. TAKAGO NATURE PATH —— M

Course: Kisarazu Station (by bus) → Toyofusa → Mt. Takago → Seiwachū Bus Stop (by bus) → Kisarazu Station

Reference map: Kinadayama (鬼泪山) and Sakahata (坂畑) 1:25,000 Sheet Maps.

Walking time: About 4 hours.

Points of interest: Mixed forests that are home to Japanese monkeys, numerous wildflowers, superb views from the summit of Mt. Takago, and Takago Kannon Temple.

GETTING THERE

From Platform 4 of Tokyo Station, catch a rapid service train (*kaisoku*, 快速) on the JR Uchibō Line (内房線) bound for Kimitsu (君津), and get off at Kisarazu (木更津) Station (about 1 hour 25 minutes). Rapid service trains leave infrequently, but faster (just over 1 hour), more comfortable, and more expensive (¥930 surcharge) limited expresses (*tokkyū*, 特急) also depart from Platform 2 or 3, mostly for Tateyama (館山). Again, you should get off at Kisarazu. (These platform numbers refer to the underground platforms at Tokyo Station.)

If none of the above is convenient, it is possible to take any of the regular JR Yokosuka Line (横須賀線) trains from Platforms 2, 3 or 4, depending on the time, to Chiba (千葉). It is also possible from Shinjuku Station (Platform 9) to take JR Sōbu Line (総武線) trains to Chiba. These require about 45 minutes and 1 hour 10 minutes, respectively. At Chiba, catch a local train (Kimitsu, Tateyama, or Awakamogawa, 安房鴨川, destinations) on the Uchibō Line to Kisarazu (40–53 minutes).

In all cases, the basic ticket (excluding any surcharge) costs ¥1,420.

Pass through the ticket barrier of Kisarazu Station, turn left, and walk down the steps to Bus Stand No. 4, where you should

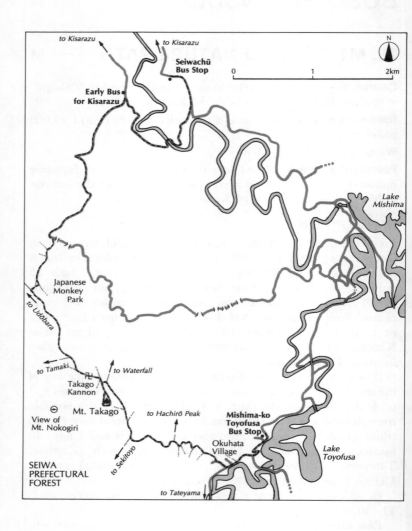

board the bus for Mishima-ko/Toyofusa (三島湖 豊英). The latter stages of the ride are quite scenic, as the bus passes Lake Mishima. Get off at the terminus, about 1 hour 10 minutes later. The fare is ¥920.

From Toyofusa to Mt. Takago (1 hour 40 minutes)

From the left side of the road at the bend near the bus stop are good views of one part of Lake Toyofusa. Note that care is needed here and in many other places along this walk, due to the steep precipices that border the route. The ubiquitous dandelion and curved-top *tennanshō* (*Arisaema*) plants grow along or just off the edges of this road.

Walking in the same direction as the bus was traveling, turn right a few meters past a hiking map board after approximately 10 minutes, into Okuhata Village. This is the second road beyond the small cemetery path cut into the roadside embankment.

After passing between fields and houses for a few hundred meters, turn right at a bend up the steps marked "Takago Kannon, Hachirō Peak" (高宕観音 八良塚). This old hollowed-out path, now known as the "Mt. Takago Nature Path" (高宕自然遊歩道), initially ascends a fairly steep slope covered with ferns and spring wildflowers including blue-purple *hotarukazura* (gromwell or puccoon), small white *tsurukanokosō* (valerian), and various white, pink, and mauve *sumire* (violet), but it soon flattens out. Ignore small paths leading off. The main path crosses several log "bridges" and provides good views of the surrounding forested hills that are home to many kites.

The trail begins to climb again and 35–40 minutes after leaving Okuhata enters relatively dark, dense forest near a junction beside which is a bench. Depending on the time, you can lunch here or else at the summit of Mt. Takago. The path to the right leads to Hachirō Peak (八良塚), about 20 minutes away. For those wishing to scale this, a picnic table and seats can be found near the top. There are good views from this point, but the summit is not interesting in itself. In addition, beautiful pink *tsutsuji* (azalea) flowers bloom in spring on cliffs along the edges of this path, as well as on parts of the main trail described in this walk.

To continue the main walk, proceed straight through this intersection, past the right-hand path to Hachirō Peak, toward Takago Kannon Temple(高宕観音). After 10–15 minutes, turn right toward Takago Kannon, that is, away from Sekitoyo (関豊). This mixed forest contains a great variety of trees, such as maple and *himeaoki* (laurel), as well as many birds. In summer, *ajisai* (hydrangea) is common. Beware of precipices along the side of the path.

About 30 minutes later, after passing through a plantation, turn left toward Takago Kannon and the summit of Mt. Takago (高宕観音 高宕山頂). The path to the right follows a small stream to a waterfall, (大滝). After 50 meters, turn left, again toward the summit of Mt. Takago (*Takago-san*), which is only 10 minutes away. If you find the last part of the climb a little daunting due to the adjacent sheer drop, take the rather overgrown alternative route to the left, which begins about halfway up. The path is flanked at one point by *tsubaki* (camellia) trees that have pink flowers in spring. The 315-meter-high summit is only big enough for a few people, but it provides outstanding views of mountain ranges in all directions, as well as of the native forest where wild *sakura* (cherry) trees flourish. On especially clear days, Tokyo Bay and Mt. Fuji are visible.

From Mt. Takago to Seiwachū Bus Stop (2 hours 20 minutes)

Returning to the first of the two nearest junctions, continue straight ahead, toward Takago Kannon. A few minutes later, turn left into the tunnel carved through the rock. At the bottom of this entrance is Takago Kannon, an old temple dedicated to the Goddess of Mercy (Kannon). The balcony of this predominantly timber structure, built on a ledge extended by carving a large niche out of the soft rock, is a good place for a rest. Leave by the main entrance down the old stone steps, past stone guardian figures that include *koma inu* (mythical Korean dogs). *Shaga* (fringed iris) flowers adorn the sides of this path in spring.

An excellent but somewhat overgrown alternative route from here is to take the second (unmarked) track to the left after leaving Takago Kannon. This little used and old trail, perhaps best for experienced walkers, descends to a small stream, from where the going gets a little tougher. The stream becomes larger, and runs

Lake Toyofusa, as seen from
the start of the walk.

through a beautiful gorge with a high, sheer rock face on one side.
In some places, you have to walk in the stream, but eventually the
autumn *rindō* (gentian)-fringed and generally unmarked path
heads uphill, subsequently crossing streams by means of small log
bridges. Unless you take one of the paths to the left, you will eventually come out on a forest road, from where you should veer left
onto progressively larger roads until you reach the intersection
with Tamaki Eki (環駅) Bus Stop slightly to the right. The additional time (from the turnoff) for this alternative is about 3 hours.
The 25-minute bus ride to Kazusaminato (上総湊) Station on the
Uchibō Line costs ¥300. Return home using the trains already described (¥1,590, not including surcharge).

.If you don't take the alternative route, from Takago Kannon
Temple continue to follow the old ferny temple trail which, in
places, has steps cut out of the rock of the mountainside. From a
clearing farther on, you can see the side of a distant rocky cliff.
This is part of an old quarry that used to be occupied by wild
monkeys.

About 30–35 minutes from Takago Kannon, turn right toward
Mt. Ishitarō (石射太郎山), that is, away from Udōbara (宇藤原).
Climb this narrow path up and to the left along the ridge,
avoiding the many minor tracks. This entire area is known as
Nihonsaru-kōen (Japanese Monkey Park), but the monkeys move
around in this large forest, so you may not spot any. Among the
more common spring wildflowers on this slope are yellow *yamabuki*

(Japanese rose or globeflower), light-blue *murasaki* (gromwell), and small white roses.

In 15 minutes, you should reach a small building near which is a view of a rocky crag and the surrounding hills. From here, descend to the left, taking the right-hand path marked "Takago Forest Road" (高宕林道) at the nearby intersection. A later division of the path is deceptive as the two trails rejoin. The trail passes more old quarrying sites, once home to monkeys, and then goes down through a plantation before meeting a bitumen road 10–15 minutes away, near a disused tunnel. Follow this road to the left for 30–35 minutes past fields, thatch-roofed houses, and kilns to a T-junction. There are large purple *azami* (thistle), white *himeutsugi* (small-flowered deutzia), and white-and-gold *harujion* (skevish or fleabane) along the roadsides in spring.

A stop (植畑上郷) for the Kisarazu-bound bus is a few hundred meters away to the left, but the last bus leaves about 4:30 P.M. If it is already too late, go right from the T-junction instead of left. Turn left at another T-junction 25 minutes later. Some 10 minutes down this road is Seiwachū (清和中) Bus Stop on the left. The last bus passes at about 6:30 P.M. To Kisarazu costs ¥760 and takes 50–60 minutes.

Return to Tokyo from Kisarazu Station by following in reverse the instructions in the "Getting There" section for this walk.

Approach to Takago Kannon Temple.

APPENDIX

A. Suggested walks according to season

SPRING

Mt. Futago

Omote-Tanzawa Forest

Mt. Mitsumine

The Northern Takao Ridge

Mt. Tenkaku and Mt. Ōtaka

Bō Peak

Senjō Field

Mt. Takago Nature Path

SUMMER

Cape Tsurugi

Jimmu Temple

Mt. Ōgusu

The Three Peaks of Takamizu

Kami-Daima to Ogose

Myōjō Peak

Mt. Happu

AUTUMN

Mt. Takao

Mt. Kuratake

Mt. Mitake

Mt. Gozen

Nenogongen and Take Temple

WINTER

Nihonsugi Pass

Lake Tanzawa to Yaga

Tama River

Sengen Ridge

Inba Marsh

B. Five walks for the visitor with limited time

Cape Tsurugi
The Northern Takao Ridge
Mt. Gozen
Senjō Field
Mt. Takago Nature Path

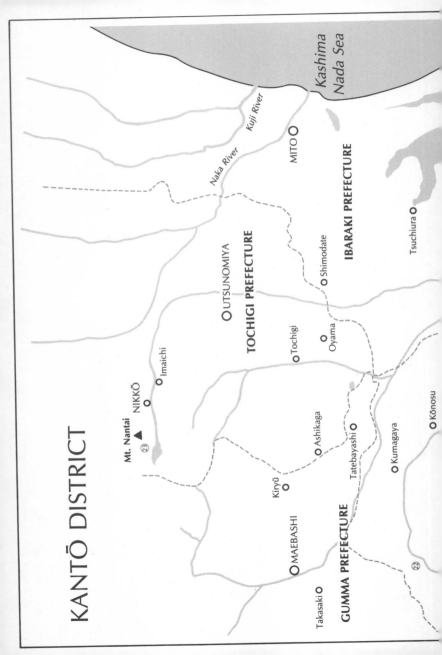